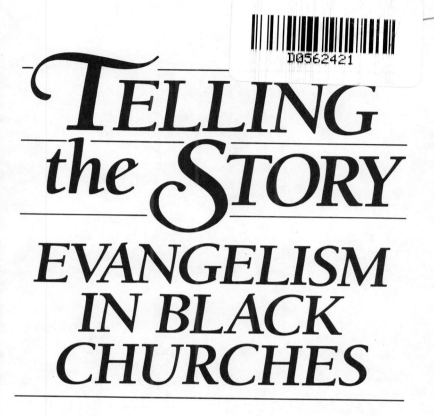

TELLING the STORY

EVANGELISM IN BLACK CHURCHES

JAMES O. STALLINGS

FOREWORD BY JAMES MELVIN WASHINGTON

Judson Press ® Valley Forge

TELLING THE STORY: EVANGELISM IN BLACK CHURCHES

Copyright © 1988
Judson Press, Valley Forge, PA 19482-0851

Third Printing, 1991

The Scripture quotations in this publication are from the Revised Standard Version of the Bible, copyrighted 1946, 1952 © 1971, 1973 by the Division of Christian Education of the National Council of the Churches of Christ in the U.S.A., and used by permission.

LIBRARY OF CONGRESS
Library of Congress Cataloging-in-Publication Data

Stallings, James O.
    Telling the story : evangelism in black churches / James O. Stallings.
        p. cm.
    ISBN 0-8170-1124-2
    1. Evangelistic work—United States. 2. Afro-American churches.
3. Afro-Americans—Religion. I. Title.
BV3773.S68 1988
269'.2'08996073—dc19   88-559
                                    CIP

The name JUDSON PRESS is registered as a trademark in the U.S. Patent Office.
Printed in the U.S.A.

Contents

James Stallings is a member of the Evangelism staff of the Board of National Ministries, American Baptist Churches. His skills and background have been highly valued in his seven years on our staff. He also serves to keep us honest in our understanding of the high degree of racial ethnic diversity in our denomination and hence, the need to internalize that understanding in developing resources for evangelism, growth, and renewal. As part of "The Growing Church" emphasis with which the Evangelism staff has been working for these last eight years, this resource has been prepared.

Clearly the book is written for black churches. Careful research has gone into learning the story of Christianity in black America and its failures and triumphs. I know of no other place where this story of evangelism is told, certainly not this well. In one sense Stallings picks up all the fragments of the whole story that started as oral tradition. Now it is an excellent historical record written primarily to give clues to the style of evangelism that is indigenous to black churches. But the story is also power-full, motivating black churches to the continuing ministry of telling the Good News. It should have wide reading in all black churches.

But it is a story for whites as well. As I read it my heart was warmed (and many times sorrowed) and my understanding of the roots of black religion and its marvelous expression in America immensely expanded in reading the trials blacks have faced in their sojourn here.

For all of us there are transferable concepts usable for evangelism. Good News must always be good news for the whole person. Personal and social witness were not meant to be separated. The Good News must be contextualized in order to be heard, and churchly practice must use the symbols of the culture of the people if it is to maintain its vitality. Surely we must know the story of Jesus and his love, but we must know *our* story, too. In sharing both, people will find *their own* story.

Emmett V. Johnson
Director of Evangelism
American Baptist Churches
USA

Foreword

*T*his book represents one of the first attempts to use narrative theology to describe, interpret, and suggest strategies for Afro-American evangelism. The title, *Telling the Story,* might sound like the use of another cliche that a lazy author would use to disguise the fact that patient historical and theological analysis are absent from the text. Nothing could be further from the truth in regard to Jim Stallings's work. In six succinct chapters he succeeds admirably well in condensing a large array of useful information and fine insights into a readable form for both clergy and laity concerned with the salvation, revitalization, and nurture of those who need to confess that Jesus is indeed the Christ.

Stallings is especially concerned with those souls whose foreparents experienced slavery as recently as the last century. They have a peculiar set of spiritual and material sufferings that have required (and still require) different evangelistic practices. He exegetes why that is the case by arguing, in the spirit of H. Richard Niebuhr's *The Meaning of Revelation,* that evangelism is essentially focusing our individual stories in such a way that they disclose God's grace and celebrate our communal roots.

The pseudo-universalism and imperialism of so much of Western and American Christianity's past assumed the necessity to commit the cultural emasculation of those whose backgrounds were not White Anglo-Saxon Protestant. This often led to confusing conversion with cultural regeneration. The more Protestants identified with the dominant culture, the more they embraced the dangers of both idolatry and complicity in maintaining an oppressive status quo. This became increasingly true as industrial capitalism seized the allegiance of the Protestant establishment in the late nineteenth century. Its fidelity to what Thorstein Veblen called "conspicuous consumption," profiteering, and labor exploitation, was, as the tiny band of social gospel prophets correctly foresaw, a blatant assault against the major tenets of the kingdom of God. Moreover, this new form of the Christian identification with the social order meant that *evangelization* became *evangelism*. The desire and need to proselytize succumbed to the forces of commodification and Western expansionism.

Modern Revivalism employed sales tactics that had no biblical basis. Many evangelical Christians led the way in this new form of practical infidelity, unwittingly contributing to the modern effort to render a gospel that had lowly origins banal and impotent. But alienation has been the unwitting consequence, burden, and asset of religious and secular technological evangels. Those on the margins of the Protestant hegemony saw this more clearly than benevolent liberal evangelicals who were struggling to maintain the old consensus. The old evangelical phalanx found themselves in the post-Reconstruction period in an increasingly pluralistic America seemingly overwhelmed by three new forces: 1) racism and the challenge of the persistent demand for self-determination from an emerging black middle class, 2) a tidal wave of European immigrants, and 3) the cultural changes and deeply nihilistic consequences of the emergence of British forms of industrial capitalism in the United States. The marginalized had no genetic moral superiority. Their moral authority was situational rather than ontological. They were more desperate for existential power than those at the center of power. The gospel message with its favoritism toward the oppressed attracted many of the most alienated denizens of the republic. Those whose citizenship rights were either minimal or stolen needed to hear that they could become citizens of a kingdom whose full dawning lay in the immediate future. Many of them refused to embrace despair. Those who kept their sanity believed they belonged to an *aristocracy of faith*. Indeed, many of them believed that their encounter with the modern absurdities of racism made them part of a favored spiritual genealogy that extended far into the ancient African and Hebrew past. They were not the only ones to believe this, however. Many of their white oppressors also believed this.

The unfortunate Anglo-Saxonism that infused so much of the white liberal evangelical circles hampered their ability to respond to the need to particularize the gospel in the emerging pluralistic context of the decolonized post-1945 world. The sad general disregard for the past histories of ancient peoples in general, and most especially the histories of Africans, did not prepare the beneficiaries of European and American colonialism to share power with the Two-Thirds World. This general abysmal ignorance was compounded in Christendom whose supercilious theological convictions and cultural practices did not equip them to learn about the history and theology of the black Christian tradition. Those who are still victimized by this outlook will merely ignore this book. Racism is a great cancer within the Body of Christ.

Evangelism has in recent times fallen prey to the limitations of technology. Sunshine faces beam cosmetic images of fabricated joy and peace for a society that thrives upon stimulation. The spirit is invoked on cue. Some complained, as I have already indicated, in earlier times about establishing the ritual among American Protestants of making 11 A.M. on Sundays the "appointed hour." It seemed odious to drag the Holy Spirit into the process of making a fetish out of our fabricated notions of time. David S. Landes makes it clear, as suggested by the title of his book *Revolution in Time: Clocks and the Making of the Modern World,* that the ruthless but beneficial cauldron of an industrial-capitalist order demanded that labor be measured in order to have a cost accounting of every hour. I call this development the "commodification of the body" because it valued the worth of human beings according to the speed with which they could move their bodies across a specified amount of space within a specific amount of time. In religious worship, such demarcation of time may indeed seem efficient, but it certainly has the effect of dampening any spiritual fires that threaten to disrupt our sedate and limited appointments with God on Sunday morning.

But the higher calling the Afro-American tradition of evangelism illustrates is that the universality of the gospel is a by-product of our particular experiences. Hegemonic claims that one tradition or one interpretation of the Christian story is or ought to be normative forecloses the immense ingenuity of God's salvific vocation. Past attempts to link evangelism with cultural homogeneity overlooked the implied theological conflict between God as Creator and God as Savior. How can the Creator create within the same species creatures whose sins are ontological rather than situational? This proposition offends human conceptions of justice. Indeed, it defies logic even if it is true. Glib answers elude us. We are left with a mystery.

Stallings helps us to see that as we refine our tools to offer and practice the liberation of Christian testimony we are also in need of more humility about what we can claim about God's vocation to save and reconcile. If we can be reconciled with God through the act of confession, the patient revolution required and wrought by conversion can lead to a more complete embrace of the seemingly progressive sanctification that bids us come and embrace the more abundant life. This requires submitting our ideologies to the awesome and worthy scrutiny of our Lord Jesus as he looks down upon us, and bids our faithful Creator to "forgive us" because we really do not know what we are doing when we make a fixation out of our mundane commitments and tribal loyalties.

James Melvin Washington, Ph.D.
Professor of Church History
Union Theological Seminary
(N.Y.)

Preface

S tories come in all sizes, shapes, and forms, and all sorts of circumstances. They are really gifts from God speaking to us, allowing us if we listen to hear, see, grow, and be transformed. Hopefully, I'm learning to always be present for these special moments that a friend and colleague describes as "holy nudges."

This book is about stories—personal, cultural, and *God's*. It is about what uniquely happens in the life of a people when their story connects with God's story and the Word becomes flesh "living among us" (John 1:14, *The Jerusalem Bible*). It is a book about evangelism that must always tell the story of God's loving and liberating activity in the lives of people and in the world through Jesus Christ.

This book will review the unique tradition of evangelism in black churches for the recovery of their story. The story will be examined for its meaning—its world view. The tradition will be questioned for its contemporary significance for ministry, especially evangelism. In Chapters 2 and 3, a survey of evangelism in black churches from their inception until the early twentieth century will be given. Chapter 4 will concentrate on the oral tradition for explicating the evangelistic lifestyle. The meaning of the story will be investigated in Chapter 5 for unearthing the major themes in the community story. Finally, in Chapter 6, I will look at the new context of the story, the current crises over identity, and the need to renew the story, places of mission, and the challenge of ministry today and tomorrow.

Like so many projects this book has had many twists and turns. When discussions were first held about being more intentional on resourcing black American Baptist churches, nothing such as this was even in mind. The American Baptist Evangelism Team did what all good church people do—they appointed a committee. I was staff to that committee.

When the committee met we were fortunate to hear the story of a tradition, a legacy richer than most of us ever imagined. Our committee, composed of pastors, seminary professors, seminary students, and denominational staff, scarcely recognized the scope of our inquiry. Thanks to the prodigious scholarship of Dr. James M. Washington, who led the discussions for our days together, we at last began to get a glimpse of the givenness of this sacred task.

This story could go on for some time in that three years have passed between original discussions and completion of this volume. I did not set out to write this volume, and yet in all the twists and turns the words of a committee member had the prescience of prophecy: "Jim, you will have to do it." Overwhelmed by a feeling of gross inadequacy, which I have come to know only as I engage in the preaching enterprise, I assumed this responsibility. Who am I to write such a book? What can I possibly say, significantly, on such a crucial theme? I approached this task with fear and trembling, ever mindful that all we do is inadequate and subject to judgment. Yet sometimes in our folly, God's redemptive grace is present. It is my prayer that in the foolishness of this effort, God's grace will be present and all the twists and turns of this volume will abound to the glory of God.

My debts in this enterprise are numerous. Many people have contributed to the completion of this volume. I owe immeasurably Dr. Sandy Dwayne Martin, assistant professor of Church History at The Interdenominational Theological Center in Atlanta, Georgia, for his skill and knowledge of church history and for his research and assistance in writing Chapters 2 and 3. I owe members of the committee—the Rev. Arlee Griffin, Dr. Ella P. Mitchell, Dr. Joe S. Ratliff, the Rev. Gershon Roebuck, and the Rev. Michael Turner—whose interest and advice were crucial at an early stage. A special word of thanks goes to Dr. James M. Washington, a committee member whose excitement about this project was infectious and whose counsel and advice tutored us all, especially me. Thanks go to Dr. Emmett V. Johnson, director of evangelism for American Baptist Churches in the U.S.A., whose willingness to be open to "holy nudges" has made this work possible. For the aid of my colleagues on the evangelism staff of American Baptist Churches in the U.S.A. who read this manuscript and made helpful comments, I continually am grateful.

Dr. Evans E. Crawford has been my friend and mentor for some time. His words of encouragement were constant as were his insightful comments on the manuscript. My colleagues the Rev. Tyrone E. Kilgoe and the Rev. Marsha Woodard read and reread the manuscript, offered advice, and posed difficult questions. I have grown to depend on their comradery and friendship. Ms. Madeline Williams, manager of Word Management, made a difficult task more bearable with her direction in preparation of the manuscript. I am also indebted to Ms. Sandy Ruud, who did the transcription of the cassettes for this manuscript. Ms. Kristy Arnesen Pullen, Ms. Laura Alden, and Tim Scott, editors for Judson Press, have been helpful and gently firm with this author. My thanks go to Ms. Valeria Horne and Ms. Dawn Whitaker, my secretaries who searched for books and shielded me during the writing of this manuscript. To John Savage, who years ago taught me to appreciate the value of story, I say thanks. I could not end without expressing an abiding word of thanks to my mother, Mrs. Dora A. Davis, whose stories excited me at a very early age and whose prayers sustained me even until now; and to my sister, Mrs. Catherine Stallings-Luckett, whose discussion of the concept of story helped me to flesh out my own ideas.

While my debts are many and the advice has been generous, I am solely responsible for the scope and direction of this book. If in your reading the written word does not communicate the passion in my heart, I hope you will remember that I am still learning to be present for "the holy nudges."

CHAPTER *1*

Why Story?

Some years ago during an evangelism seminar with a group of black local church leaders in North Carolina, I asked each participant to reflect on his or her faith pilgrimage to recall those times when each was certain of God's involvement in his or her life. Two interesting things happened. An elderly gentleman in the group had resisted following the instructions for this activity for two sessions. I could not understand why. In a discussion with him, he began to share a powerful story of some events many years before that had been very traumatic and yet during which he was sure of God's providential care in being delivered from an intense racial confrontation. He indicated he had not spoken of that experience in over fifty years—not even to his wife. His emotions, upon the telling, could not be contained.

Each evening, during the worship service, someone was asked to share his or her own testimony with worshipers. Midweek one of the group's participants shared a testimony quite unlike any usually heard in black worship services. She observed, "I know you have never heard a testimony like this one before, but I have been learning how to tell my own story and *this is my story.*"

I left North Carolina convinced that something of significance had occurred for both of these people. I still can remember the intense emotion and power with which the elderly church deacon shared his personal encounter and the vitality of the young lady who proudly exclaimed, "I'm telling my story."

In many settings since then I have continued to help people tell their own stories. I have heard many stories, yet each one has been different and all have been extraordinary.

In listening to and reflecting on them I have made several discoveries.

1. The stories being told were all fragmentary, and yet in each there were strains or themes to indicate they were part of a larger story.
2. Taken together the stories reflect God's dealing with human beings—but more than just that, they tell a larger story of God's saving activity happening in the lives of men and women. It was the Christian story becoming flesh and blood and sinew.
3. For the black church steeped in the oral tradition, stories function as a vital link for passing on tradition.
4. In these stories were clues to an evangelistic lifestyle within black churches.

Story as Tradition

Telling the Story is a book about evangelism in the black church tradition and the use of story as a primary vehicle for sharing that tradition. By tradition I am referring to a network of beliefs, attitudes, and ideals that are passed down through generations.

Every community has some medium to transmit its collective character. From the beginning of time, story has been used to pass on the beliefs, attitudes, and ideals to succeeding generations. Such transmission is not neutral. Passing on the collective character from one generation to the next was a way of preserving reality or the world

view as that culture perceived it. We commonly understand this method as oral tradition. Afro-Americans have
made primary use of this medium to pass on their collective character to succeeding generations.

Story here means a narrative account of certain events.
It is more than just an account—it is an imaginative way
of ordering our experience. (I make a distinction between
imaginative and imaginary. The imaginary represents
that which is unreal while the imaginative represents the
creative, constructive powers of the mind. More discussions of this will appear in Chapter 5.) "Story," James
Cone notes, "is the history of individuals coming together
in the struggle to shape life according to commonly held
values."[1] Thus story is the possession of a community. It
possesses its own language that provides a sense of the
community's reality. While there are personal stories,
they are personal only to the extent that the individual
who lives out his or her experience in a community is
shaped by that community while at the same time the
individual participates in the shaping of the community.
The personal story is fragmentary. The community story
is the sum of the personal stories and more.

History is a species of story—thus story is related to
time. However, it is lived. It evolves from the lives of
people and not from some detached literary work. It pre-
serves the memory of past events so that those events
have meaning and power. It has a plot or plan of action.
Events in the story are ordered in such a way as to make
sense of life. The plot says something about the meaning
of life or the lack of it.

The Bible is a story. It is the story of God's loving and
redeeming activity down through history for humankind.
In the Bible the early Christian story is found in the Old
and New Testaments, with the emphasis on the latter as
the fulfillment of the former.

All people have a story. The story of Euro-Americans is
found in the history of European settlement of the North
American continent and the founding of a new nation.
The black American story is told through the songs, tales,
and narratives of African slaves and their descendants as
they sought to survive in a land hostile to their existence.

As a people tell their story, they say something to themselves, their children, and the world about how they think and live.

The black American community is a story-shaped community. Its self-understanding, language, beliefs, attitudes, and ideals are passed from one generation to another through story. Black Americans sing, play, learn, love, hate, despair, and hope through story. It is the form of all communication, whether serious or playful. In the black American community dreams, memories, anticipation, frustrations, beliefs, rumors, and even gossip are experienced or spoken in narrative. Any study of black life must begin with story.

Black Christianity

Since its emergence in the eighteenth century as a separate entity in American religious life, the black church movement has represented a clear theological, spiritual, and cultural departure from the faith community shaped by Euro-American experience. In a blending of the African heritage, the struggle for freedom with eighteenth-century Protestant evangelical fervor, the black church movement developed a unique network of beliefs, attitudes, and ideals that shaped and continued to shape its life. (In using the term "evangelical," I make a distinction between early Protestant evangelicalism and the current usages of the term that refer, essentially, to a version of fundamentalism.

The theological, spiritual, and cultural departure by black Christians has not always been recognized by whites or even some blacks. All too frequently persons, regardless of their ilk, have tried to force upon the black church movement an understanding of theology and missions alien to its own experience. Many persons have assumed that the division in God's church along color lines is superficial and can be bridged by earnest efforts in both communities. The divisions between the black church movement and its Euro-American counterpart run deeper than simply color. These appeals for unity generally have been based on the assumption that black churches are the product of an aberration in Euro-American Christianity—racism. Overcoming racism, it has been believed, would surely bring black churches back where they have always belonged. In countless settings in many ways the expression is heard, "We are really no different. We are all Christians."

Such attitudes fail to acknowledge the great diversity that existed in Euro-American Christianity that cannot be laid at the foot of racism. Failing to acknowledge its own diversity, it is easy to see how many in the Euro-American church movement also failed to see that the black church movement was and is God's mission to a community whose heritage and culture have been different.

Diversity has a long though not always glorious history in the Christian tradition. Among the several New Testament images of the church, Paul's "body of Christ" image highlights the rich diversity of the family of God. Paul, in his descriptive language to the church at Corinth, clearly sees a unity that transcends diversity. Here diversity is seen as an expression of God's generosity to the human family.

Peter's revelatory experience on the rooftop, while paving the way for the resolution of the controversy over circumcision, also demonstrated God's pleasure with diversity. What often in the American Christian community is viewed as appeals for unity are really calls for cultural uniformity.

The emphasis here on diversity in American religious life must not be understood as an attempt to widen the gulf already experienced in the family of God. Rather, it should be viewed as an attempt to help a particular community recall its own history with God; to remember those times when God's deliverance was sure and God's providential care was all-sustaining. To highlight that is to recall that experience for celebration, theologizing, planning, and program development. On the other hand, to ignore one's experience of God, to denigrate that experience and refuse to tell the story of it, to accept someone else's experience of God as more efficacious than one's own, is to demean God and one's experience of God. It is an abuse of the sacred encounter between the human personality and God and blasphemy against God. Recognition of one's own tradition and legacy does not negate other traditions or legacies.

The Need for Tradition

If we neglect the precious heritage of a healthy religious tradition, we do so at our peril. There are several ways in which a religious tradition functions positively for black churches. First, it provides a means of identity by relating a person's convictions and aspirations to a stream of ideas, people, institutions, and movements that reach back into the past and stretch forward to the future. Tradition provides a world view that includes a network of explanations that embody the ultimate assumptions through which we understand our reality. Tradition draws these assumptions and explanations into a whole and expresses them through stories, songs, sermons, creeds, worship, moral insights, tracts, and theological treatises. It also furnishes us with a moral and intellectual scale for evaluating our behavior and goals and for assessing new ideas and understandings. Tradition provides psychological and social support to cope with the great moral crises of life. In times of great anxiety, a healthy tradition provides invaluable means for sustaining a fragile existence. During birth, puberty, marriage, illness, old age, and death, a tradition can provide through its members, rituals, and intellectual resources, a rich fund of experience, illuminations, and hope to draw on. Those who ignore this do so at their own peril.

Additionally, the tradition acts as a womb for the creation of new ideas and fresh construction in theology. With great emphasis on diversity, tradition becomes a tool for progress. Those who have no tradition of thought to share with other Christians come to the table barren. What creativity one brings requires a context for development. People do not become Christians in a vacuum.

Finally, a sound tradition will save black churches from extremism. It will nurture them in their core beliefs, thus providing balance and depth to their vision of God and the world. It will give their children room to breathe and grow spiritually. It will transmit a wisdom that spans the ages. It will inspire patience to grapple with those tangled, muddled, and demanding issues that each generation must face in its own unique context. It will provide a bulwark against the incipient secularism that always threatens the people of God.

Evangelism in Black Churches

Many readers will agree with my evaluation of tradition, but they may question how it applies to evangelism. In fact, they will wonder whether there is any such thing as a tradition of evangelism in black churches. If there is, how does it differ from evangelistic activity in white churches? What, they will ask, are the origins of such a tradition? How does it inform the mission programs of black churches? Does the evangelistic task of these churches differ from its other ministries? For others the confusion over the various definitions of evangelism will cloud the picture, while some will hasten to comment on the negative image of evangelism.

All of these concerns are important. What cannot be denied, however, is that there is a definite tradition of evangelism in black churches. By evangelism I mean the activity in black churches and their mission organizations of communicating God's saving and liberating activity among men and women; calling them into community with other Christians for freedom, growth, and wholeness.

There is a growing body of material detailing at length the early religious activity of African slaves and their descendants. Albert J. Raboteau suggests, "it is possible that a few enslaved Africans may have had some contact with Christianity in their homeland."[2] Portuguese missionaries were present on the West Coast of Africa from the early sixteenth century. However, their efforts, like those of their white North American counterparts a century or two later, met with little success. Christians in North America made conversion of African slaves a high priority. For a number of reasons, one of which included the institution of slavery, spreading the gospel to slaves was a failure. Lawrence Jones concludes, "the central reason for the failure of the mission to the slaves lies mainly in the inability of these blacks to reconcile the faith of the evangelizers with their conduct." Jones says, "many . . . involved in the founding of these churches were preeminently evangelists deeply committed to the truth of the Gospel and zealous to communicate it to those that had not heard it."[3] It is clear that the work of spreading the gospel to African slaves primarily was done early by black preachers and later through activity of black churches.

Active participation by black preachers was one of the charges made against the fervor of the Great Awakening by its critics. Charles Chauncey would note " . . . yea Negroes, have taken upon them to do the Business of Preachers."[4] Eighteenth-century evangelists preached to racially mixed congregations and had little doubt about the capacity of slaves to share in the conversion experience. Many included black preachers in their revival meetings. These early preachers would go on to establish churches and continue their work preaching the gospel of spiritual freedom to slaves.

The pioneers of the tradition saw their mission as more than just preaching the gospel to their brothers and sisters who had not heard. Though small in number they did not separate their interior institutional life from its mission in and on behalf of the world. They believed that their mission consisted of the task of freeing black folks' souls from sin and their bodies from physical, political, and social oppression, and of setting the conditions of existence so that they could achieve their full humanity. It was for them a special call from God thrust upon them that was different from that of their white counterparts. From these simple beginnings came a movement that now is called the black church movement.

CHAPTER 2

Recovery of the Story: Black Churches and Evangelism

*T*he purpose of this chapter is to recover the foundational story of evangelism in the black churches. As always with story no attempt will be made to provide a detailed, statistical account of evangelists and missionaries, a chronological listing of the numbers of converts to the various churches, or the number of churches initiated as a result of evangelistic activities. Rather, the story will examine the meaning that evangelism has had for the black churches in America. It also will outline methods of evangelistic outreach and the impact they have had upon the church.

Evangelism, as I have already noted, includes all activity and methods in black churches, institutional and invisible, through which God's saving and liberating activity in Jesus Christ among men and women was communicated; calling them into community with other Christians for wholeness, growth, and freedom. This outreach activity takes on various forms: evangelistic and revival preaching, missionary-oriented education, commissioning of persons to establish or organize new churches in the U.S. and abroad, and sharing of one's stories with another. Some methods may be classified as formal because they are part of an institutional structure explicitly committed to enhancing church growth (for example, a denominational agency or department of missions). At other times, however, the methods manifest themselves in more infor-

Def. of evange

mal ways—activities that arise in a more spontaneous manner or that arise incidental to other efforts (for example, persons converted in a context of an educational institution devoted to moral training or persons converted through experiences that were influenced by the sharing of one individual with another).

The second term to be defined or clarified is black church(es). By the "black church" I refer to those congregations and denominations populated mainly by Afro-Americans and whose activities, at least at the very immediate levels, are operated by and controlled by blacks. This definition includes the congregations that compose predominantly black denominations, such as the National Baptist Convention, USA, Inc., the National Baptist Convention of America, the Progressive National Baptist Convention, the African Methodist Episcopal, the African Methodist Episcopal Zion, the Christian Methodist Episcopal church, and the Church of God in Christ, as well as the predominantly black congregations (usually under the leadership of a black minister) in mainly white denominations such as the American Baptist Churches in the U.S.A., the Southern Baptist Convention, and the United Methodist church. It is necessary to classify the second group of congregations because they often have a close affinity with the first group based upon commonalities in worship style, theological outlook, and proximity to or presence within the general black community. With or without any of the first-mentioned characteristics, these congregations invariably become "black" for all practical purposes because of the commonality of black experiences in such a color-conscious society.

This story focuses mainly upon churches within the independent black denominations. There is absolutely no intention to ignore or marginalize the important historical role of the other churches. Rather, the focus has more to do with concerns of manageability and stewardship of time. Black Christians exercised far more control over the planning and operations of the independent churches since they controlled the denominations as well as their constituent operations. Equally, if not more significantly, the independent black denominations have in the past and do at the present contain the overwhelming majority of black Christians. Blacks held in slavery were for the most part prohibited from establishing their own churches as well as prevented from affiliating themselves with independent black denominations. Interestingly, upon achieving freedom during and at the conclusion of the Civil War, these ex-slaves either flocked to the independent denominations in massive numbers or formed their own separate churches, as shall be observed in the following pages.

Finally, by way of introduction, this story chiefly chronicles and analyzes events between roughly 1750 and 1930. In addition, this period represents the movement of the black church "from slavery to freedom." During these years blacks, once excluded from the Christian fellowship in the United States, embraced the faith, established separate religious institutions, endured the dehumanizing system of slavery by finding true personhood and worth in Christianity, emerged from slavery, formed regional and national organizations, solidified the institutionalization of their denominations, and boldly spread their presence abroad.

Evangelism in the History of Christianity

We must acknowledge that the activities of evangelism and the black church movement did not occur in a theological, social, or historical vacuum. The church is the people of God, the body of Christ, who have been called into community by the saving, liberating work of God in Jesus Christ. Its fellowship has been empowered by the Holy Spirit for engagement in mission within the world. Mission involves everything the church does: proclaiming the gospel of the kingdom of God and being involved in activity to liberate humankind from spiritual, social, psychological, physical and economic bondage. All are included in the mission of the church. Evangelism therefore is mission, part of comprehensive mission of the church. Mission, however, is more than evangelism.

The history of evangelism in the Christian church is well documented. It is not my purpose to review a prodigious body of literature here. Rather, notation is made to acknowledge those movements and strains of thought that clearly influence the historical and theological development of the traditions of the black church. I have already noted earlier that the black church movement in the United States represented a unique blending of African cultural heritage and the struggle for liberation with seventeenth- and eighteenth-century evangelical Christianity.

Sixteenth-Century Protestant Reformation

Beginning in the 1500s a very significant movement entered upon the stage of European Christianity: the Protestant Reformation, in which many Christians in western, central, and northern Europe broke away from the Roman Catholic Church. The Reformation had its forerunners in personalities (such as John Wyclif of England) who antedated the movement by a few centuries. The most immediate powerful human inspiration, however, came through the writings, preaching, and ecclesiological activities of German priest Martin Luther, whose influence began in 1517. It is essential to understand the ramifications of the Protestant Reformation for evangelism. Leaders such as Martin Luther, John Calvin, and Ulrich Zwingli and the churches that emerged as a result of their activities were often termed "evangelical." As time passed the reformers increasingly envisioned the Roman Catholic Church as having lost touch with true, authentic, biblical, and apostolic Christianity. The reformers saw themselves, on the other hand, as preaching the true religion of Christ. They believed that they brought good news to people for whom it had long been buried under countless rituals, customs, Scriptures written in a foreign language, and laws and regulations that too often enslaved people to the hierarchy and hypocrisy of the Roman Catholic Church rather than freeing them in the grace of Christ. Despite significant differences among themselves that prevented institutional unity, each group of reformers understood their mission as preaching the gospel of Christ that God welcomes sinners not on the basis of their works, but on the basis of justification by faith.

Obviously, the Roman Catholic Church disagreed vigorously with much of the reformers' theology and the criticisms leveled against it by the Reformation churches. Indeed, the Roman Catholic Church insisted that it was the one true church, had sole authority to interpret Scripture, and branded the dissidents as "heretic" preachers of false doctrine. But Catholics did more than merely reaffirm their churchly traditions. Individuals and movements in the church, as in times past, called for renewal from within the Catholic body. The Society of Jesus, or Jesuits, founded by Ignatius of Loyola, vigorously defended the office of the pope and Catholic doctrine and also initiated missionary movements that secured converts in various areas of the world, including Africa, the Americas, and India. Thus, one unwittingly positive result of the Protestant-Catholic confrontations was the inclusion of many more people into the churches as Catholics and Protestants.

Seventeenth- and Eighteenth-Century Evangelical Movements

Protestant evangelism, as has been noted, provides the most immediate context for the emergence of the black church movement. Early Protestant teachings furnished a powerful impetus for evangelism. By the mid 1600s, however, Protestantism itself had degenerated in many areas into a technical, legalistic, cold, dry formalism. This state of affairs had more in common with the sixteenth-century Protestant perception of Roman Catholicism than it had with the liberating gospel of grace preached by Luther.

In the latter quarter of the seventeenth century, a Lutheran, Philipp Jakob Spener (1635–1705), started the movement of Pietism in Germany. In his writings, Spener set forth certain principles of Christian living that not only pointed back to the early Protestant reformers but also influenced the rise of eighteenth-century evangelicalism in Europe and the Americas.[1] He advocated personal piety and individual, conscientious reading of the Bible. He called for simplicity in the teachings of Christianity rather than the complicated manner in which theologians presented it. Spener advocated that serious Christians should feel free to organize small groups for devotion. He reiterated Luther's earlier principle that each Christian was a minister of sorts in serving others and glorifying God; and clearly taught that Christian service to others should be directed to their this-worldly, material needs as well as their "soul" or "spiritual" concerns.

As time passed Pietism embraced other features that were to have significant effect on the emergence of modern Protestant emphasis upon evangelism. It introduced the idea that the faithful should be able to examine their lives and report a struggle within their souls that culminated in a conversion experience at a particular time and place. Clearly this feature of Pietism foreshadowed later revivals when sinners were called upon to flee from lives of sin and instantaneously experience in a dramatic or powerful manner the salvation of the Lord. In addition, Pietists made a great contribution to Protestantism in that they reminded the churches that the Great Commission that Jesus gave to the early apostles—to go into all of the world and preach the gospel—was obligatory for contemporary Christians. Hence, the Moravians, spiritual siblings of Pietism, became major exponents of foreign missions despite their relatively small numbers.

In the British Isles and the American colonies in the 1700s, Protestantism for many had become dry and formal with little life. Leaders appeared and movements began in these areas, often influenced by Moravian teaching and piety that called the believers back to a more fundamental, dynamic relationship with God. In Britain, John Wesley, an elder in the Church of England, became perhaps the best-known representative of the Anglican revivals. Influenced by the Moravians and the writings of Luther, Wesley, like others of the revival, traveled through the British Isles on horseback, preaching repentance in churches, in the open air, and in prisons, among other places. Wesley made a number of contributions to Christian theology that powerfully shaped much of

American and Afro-American evangelism. First, he preached an Arminian understanding of the Christian faith. Though no one could gain salvation without the promptings and assistance of God, all persons are granted a "prevenient grace" so that they may accept salvation. In other words, God provides everyone with sufficient assisting grace so they may choose salvation if they wish or they may reject God's invitation. Wesley strongly argued against the doctrine of predestination preached by many in the Protestant churches. Predestination asserted that God had elected from the foundation of the world to save some for eternal life and had either chosen others for eternal damnation or had simply refused to grant them the necessary grace by which they could elect salvation. Arminianism, once appropriated by revival preachers in early nineteenth-century America, freed them to be bolder and more persistent in obtaining conversions since it was believed possible through constant appeals to weaken the will to choose death and strengthen the will to select eternal life.

Another major and perhaps the most original contribution to the revivals in the British Isles and America was the doctrine of Christian perfection. This teaching often has been misunderstood. Wesley meant that after salvation the individual should continue to strive earnestly to know and please God. He envisioned Christian perfection as a gradual process and noted that some Christians would not achieve it this side of eternity. But the faithful Christians who were perfected would be so motivated by the love and reverence of God that they would not knowingly or deliberately sin against God. It was possible that one could inadvertently commit a sin. But once the presence of that sin was revealed to him or her, then that person would immediately repent.

This doctrine of Christian perfection was significant for American religious history for two reasons. First, it laid the foundation for the emergence of the holiness movement whose impact was in turn felt upon the emerging and predominantly black Pentecostal movement of the turn of the twentieth century. Second, perfectionism manifested itself in social terms as many American Christians sought to use the principles of the gospel in the nineteenth century to create a perfect nation under God, a nation that had eliminated slavery, abolished drunkenness, infused the principles of Christian learning—a nation that would serve as a light to the nations of God's righteousness and justice.

In the American colonies the first major thrust toward evangelism came in the form of the Great Awakening often dated between the 1720s and the 1740s. Beginning in New Jersey as a result of the preaching of Theodore J. Frelingheysen, the movement soon spread to New England and later around 1740 to the southern colonies where the greatest number of blacks—held in chattel slavery—lived. Significant and well-known participants in the awakening included Gilbert Tennent, Jonathan Edwards (the famous New England theologian), and George Whitefield, the great preacher who was also active in the Anglican Revival and at one time was a protégé of John Wesley. With its emphasis upon immediate conversion and personal fellowship with God, this series of revivals was instrumental in bringing masses of people, white and black, into the churches. This First Great Awakening exhibited features of Calvinism, with its stress on predestination. The Second Great Awakening, which began in the 1790s and extended to the 1830s, showed the impact of Wesleyan principles. Both were instrumental in securing membership of Afro-Americans; however, the second more so than the first.

It is necessary to make some statements of summary on evangelism in the history of the Christian church. First, evangelism is part of the mission of the church. Christianity historically has made its greatest strides in terms of vitality and securing members when it has engaged in evangelization.

Second, the Pietist movement's introduction of the notion of personal faith, centering on simplicity, made denominations and classes relative. Third, Wesley's contribution of the availability of salvation to everyone, along with the doctrine of Christian perfection, heavily influenced the evangelical movement in America.

Finally, some attention must be given to eighteenth-century evangelicalism. Evangelicalism is a form of Christianity that highlights personal faith. It emphasizes a conversion experience or need for the person to recall a clear, explicit decision to surrender his or her life to God. Revivals are significant tools used historically by evangelicals to call the faithful back to a more earnest Christian life and sinners away from damnation to everlasting life. In addition, great emphasis is placed upon an individual, personal relationship with God that involves private prayer, Scripture reading, (usually) a strict code of personal morality, and witnessing about God's grace to others. Evangelicals do not hesitate to proclaim that a personal encounter with Christ is the only way to salvation and thus actively seek the salvation of all Christians.

Afro-American Slaves Embrace Christianity

Several strains converged for the origins of the beginning of the story in the eighteenth century. It is important to note that the first major influx of Afro-Americans into the Christian movement occurred under the activities of the evangelicals. Some people often repeat the myth that white slaveholders forced Christianity upon slaves in order to make them more pliable. This myth bespeaks a misunderstanding or an underestimation of our black ancestors to distinguish between religion and propaganda. Second, whites for a century actually remained quite cool to the idea of Christianizing blacks.[2] There were many reasons, among them were the belief of many that blacks had no souls; fear of rebellion sparked by the egalitarian principles of Christianity; a conviction that since Christians should only enslave barbarians or "heathens," blacks should remain unbaptized; the scarcity of ministers and religious workers; and the general nonreligious, carnal atmosphere recognized in the colonies.

Between 1619 and 1740 blacks had their own reasons for rejecting the Christianity presented to them. To be succinct, we might simply acknowledge that these sons and daughters of Africa saw little value in this white version of Christianity. As stated previously, our ancestors, though chained, brutalized, and mistreated were not naive. They understood that many of the teachings directed at them were intended to secure and maintain their subjugation and oppression, not to free their bodies or their souls. Besides, a slave master with a whip who separated families and brutalized pregnant mothers was hardly the best or even an authentic representative of the Divine. In addition, we may comfortably reject the notion that all traces of their African cultures, including their religions, had been erased from their consciousness. As faint as that consciousness must have sometimes appeared in a strange and barren land, they did not see during those first hundred years any acceptable replacement.

Then came the message from the evangelicals. What McClain in his *Black People in the Methodist Church* says about the appeal of the Wesleyan message to blacks could easily be said of practically all the evangelicals—Methodists, Baptists, and Presbyterians, among others. Evangelicalism (1) contained a simple message that portrayed God's love for all who would respond to the offer of grace; (2) called forth the response of the whole person, including the emotions; (3) seemed especially suited for all people who were burdened, outcast, unpopular, and left out.[3] It would be inaccurate to select any one of these and overemphasize its influence at the expense of other explanations. Also, we must remember that the awakenings attracted not only black slaves but also free, poor whites. Evangelicalism's impact transcended all socioeconomic boundaries that normally separated people.

But the fact remains that it enlisted the participation of blacks like no other past efforts. In the context of Afro-America, it then had special appeal. The emotional character of the revivals certainly paralleled the religious experiences of possessions by the gods and spirits to which Africans had been accustomed. Mathews in *Religion in the Old South* comments upon this feature:

> A universal phenomenon of revivals in England, Wales, Ireland, New England, and Colonies to the south, the conversion experience . . . seemed to the Africans to be very much like the vitality of their own religion. . . . The conversion experience, so valued by white Evangelicals as the

primary authenticating act of their rituals, therefore, became the most important contact point between traditional African culture and the Evangelical movement. . . . That the whites believed the experience to be God's gift, and that the blacks perceived it as possession does not detract from its binding and recreating functions. . . .[4]

Mathews proceeds to illustrate other points of similarity. Incantational preaching, the rite of baptism, and the type of "enthusiastic" singing among the evangelicals were all reminiscent of African religion.[5] We could analyze quite extensively on this point. One could, of course, leave this issue of evangelical-traditional African parallels at the point of terming them as mere similarities of religious experience that aided blacks in embracing Christianity. But we could also highlight these points of contacts as a process by which Afro-Americans indigenized Christianity. That is, they accepted it in such a manner that it was placed into their thought processes and theological/ritualistic/ethical structures. We could propose that blacks took Euro-American white Christianity, baptized it in African traditional culture, and created a new Afro-American Christianity. We could go even further and propose that there are certain basic structures and experiences common in some significant degree among all religions. No people are blank sheets upon which any other people or religions can write their impressions at will. But indigenous or nature customs and thought patterns invariably become a part of the new religion, whether it is Christianity among Afro-Americans or Buddhism among the Tibetans. The long-term survival of any religion, thus, could be sociologically and anthropologically explained in part by the degree to which the religion becomes a part of the people's culture.

But we now must return to other features of evangelicalism that attracted blacks in eighteenth- and early nineteenth-century America, traits that are also treated by Mathews and McClain.[6] Blacks, even slaves, were able to participate much more freely in the evangelicalism than they could in the more formal churches that recognized a great distance between clergy and laity and made little room for poor whites, let alone black slaves. They could shout, sing, pray, and confess openly what Christ had done for them. Indeed, all persons who claimed that they had been saved were expected to do all and obligated to do some of them. In addition, some enslaved blacks performed in the role of ministers and exhorters to other slaves and sometimes to whites. I wish to emphasize that the slave system severely hampered the activities of enslaved blacks, but not to the extent that some of them could not function to a certain degree as ministers and even pastors.

Up to this point the reader may have assumed that the evangelical movement was totally white in its leadership or that the conversion of black slaves was always under the preaching of white ministers. But the awakenings, particularly in the South, were led by both whites and blacks. In many instances black-converted individuals felt God's call to become ministers to exhort others. In some instances they were able to pursue such a goal. McClain gives an account of one Henry D. Gough who, after hearing the gospel preached by the famous Methodist evangelist Francis Asbury in the late 1700s, felt deeply convicted of his sinfulness and guilty over a wasted life. It was an experience with a slave that uplifted him from his depression. McClain writes:

> Riding to one of his plantations he heard the voice of prayer and praise in a cabin, and listening, discovered that a [Negro] from a neighboring estate was leading the devotions of his own slaves, and offering fervent thanksgivings for the blessings of their depressed lot. His heart was touched, and with emotion he exclaimed, "Alas, O Lord, I have my thousands and tens of thousands, and yet ungrateful wretch that I am. I never thanked thee, as this poor slave does, who has scarcely clothes to put on or food to satisfy his hunger. . . ."[7]

We would have to read that that experience along with Asbury's preaching would have moved the plantation owner to initiate measures for the release of people he was holding in bondage, especially since they, too, were brothers and sisters in Christ with much spiritual knowledge to share with him. At any rate, we note a number of significant observations in this passage. First, blacks often held meetings among just themselves where they glorified and praised God without the assistance or guidance of whites. Second, not only did converted blacks share with one another on the same plantation but also sometimes a person "from a neighboring estate" performed the role of leader or pastor. Third, Christianity passed not only from whites to blacks but also from blacks to whites. The accounts of former slaves and slaveholders contain many references to whites, even slaveholders, not only being taught by black slave ministers but also actually experiencing conversion under their preaching and influence.

By the licensing of local and traveling preachers, relieving their work load on farms and plantations so that they might serve as pastors to their fellow slaves, and by purchasing their freedom so that blacks might preach to and pastor white and racially mixed congregations, whites sometimes cooperated (especially in the 1700s and very early 1800s) in promoting a limited degree of black religious leadership. A number of individuals took advantage of these rare opportunities.[8] Harry Hoosier, who accompanied Francis Asbury, was famous for his preaching eloquence although he was illiterate. Richard Allen, the founder of the African Methodist Episcopal church, along with his brother, was granted the opportunity to purchase his freedom and that of family members because the heart of his master had been touched by the message of an antislavery, evangelical preacher. Henry Evans became an organizer of churches for both whites and blacks in the Fayetteville, North Carolina, area in the late 1700s and early 1800s. The missionary endeavors of freeborn mulatto John Stewart indicates that religious affairs among these early evangelicals sometimes transcended the world of black and white. In the late 1700s Stewart was converted at a Methodist service after living a life of drug and alcohol addiction. Upon conversion, he became a missionary to the Wyandotte Indians in the Ohio territory. McClain credits him with having initiated home mission work within the then Methodist Episcopal church.

Historical documents attest to numerous other examples that demonstrate the multiracial character of leadership in the evangelical movement in early America (for example, Josiah Bishop, William Lemon, and John Chavis). The catechetical method of memorizing prayers, creeds, and question-answer "summaries" of the faith often skewed to the self-interest of the slaveholder at the expense of the enslaved was the primary attempt to convert black slaves before the First Great Awakening. With the advent of the latter, blacks, slaves and free, could feel some greater measure of liberty to participate and in some instances actually lead in a religious movement that did not completely relegate them to the background.

Another powerful attraction of the awakenings for blacks was the strong antislavery position that many preachers of the gospel held, especially during the early period. In many instances white slaveholders were persuaded that slavery constituted a heinous sin in the eyes of God. Some, including later preachers of the gospel such as the Baptist David Barrows and the Methodist Freeborn Garretson, were moved not only to free their slaves but also to campaign vigorously against the system. Taking their cue from the Methodist founder, John Wesley of England, and his superintendent Francis Asbury in America, courageous ministers of various denominations faced ostracism, beatings, public humiliations, and threats to their lives rather than abandon their Christian antislavery principles. Of course Methodists, Baptists, Presbyterians, and other churches had cooled their antislavery ardor considerably by the first decade of the nineteenth century. By 1810 practically all of these early white preachers who were still alive had basically conceded the long-term existence of chattel slavery. They reoriented their priorities to making sure the enslaved were presented the gospel and the enslaved's condition ameliorated where possible. This decline in antislavery fervor could be explained in a number of ways. For some, such as the Methodist Asbury, it was the realization that slaveholders would not permit the evangelization of blacks if it entailed preaching a gospel of physical freedom. For others, their socioeconomic status in life had improved over that of their poorer parents so that they, too, owned slaves. They found it impossible to labor against oppression, greed, and brutality when they were recipients of their benefits or like pleasures. Still others simply grew weary with the passage of time and changing social mores. They found it difficult to sing the Lord's songs in a strange land. Whatever the reasons and despite the decline of anti-slavery fervor among evangelicals, it remains true that many if not most of the earliest white and black evangel-ists to enslaved Afro-Americans preached a doctrine of salvation for both the body and the soul. Thus, evangeli-cal Christianity "introduced" the God who was con-cerned for the totality of the person. As we now turn our attention to evangelism within the early independent black church, we should bear in mind that this principle of holistic redemption always remained a significant ele-ment among many black Christians, slave and free.

Rise of Separate and Independent Black Churches

There are significant points we should remember in discussing the evangelistic programs and implications of the black church. First, the most successfully indepen-dent congregations and denominations flourished in northern and border states. Obviously, the existence of independent black institutions constituted a threat to slaveholders and their sympathizers. Although Andrew Bryan and others eventually were successful in organiz-ing the separate First African Baptist Church in Savan-nah, Georgia, in 1787, it was not without difficulty and was operated under the close scrutiny of the white power structure. Second, these black churches were in the pro-cess of telling their stories. A significant portion of those stories has been described by Gayraud Wilmore[9] as the "Hamitic hypothesis" and based upon what was taken as prophecy in Psalm 68:31. God had a divine plan for Afro-American Christians that they would embrace the Chris-tian faith and spread it to other sons and daughters of Africa throughout the world, particularly those on the mother continent. Not only would Afro-American Chris-tians demonstrate to white Americans the true meaning of Christian democracy, but the Christianized African race would be a light to the entire world.

Third, it must be stated that these churches were anti-slavery, that they considered chattel slavery as completely antithetical to a proper Christian lifestyle. Finally, the very existence of racially separate congregations and denominations demonstrated the prevalence of racial discrimination and prejudice inflicted upon blacks by the white-controlled religious groups. It was not unheard of for white-controlled churches to insist that blacks and whites sit separately, that blacks be served Communion after whites, that black men be barred from the ministry and/or their ministerial rank and activities be clearly circumscribed, and so forth. Many Afro-American Christians felt stifled and neglected in most mixed or white-controlled churches. Thus, the actions of leaders such as David George, George Liele, Andrew Bryan, Richard Allen, and James Varick in forming separate religious structures for black worship and devotion in and of themselves represent acts of evangelization. They were providing contexts where Afro-Americans could be more vigorously evangelized and given more authentic examples of Christian fellowship.

Although the following words of Richard Allen must not be taken to apply directly to the founding of the African Methodist Episcopal denomination in 1816, they do illustrate an earlier, firm conviction on his part that black people needed separate places of worship for evangelistic and discipleship reasons. Describing activities in 1786 Philadelphia and the racially mixed but white-controlled St. George Methodist Episcopal Church, Allen wrote:

> I soon saw a large field open in seeking and instructing my African brethren, who had been a long-forgotten people and few of them attended public worship. . . . I established prayer meetings; I raised a society in 1786 for forty-two members. I saw the necessity of erecting a place of worship for the colored people. . . .[10]

Of course, Allen met with opposition from both the prominent blacks as well as from whites associated with the Methodist Episcopal church. Nevertheless, Allen and his supporters persevered.

> We all belonged to St. George's Church—Rev. Absalom Jones, William White and Dorus Ginnings. We felt ourselves much cramped; but my dear Lord was with us, and we believed, if it was his will, the work would go on, and that we would be able to succeed in building the house of the Lord. We established prayer meetings and meetings of exhortation, and the Lord blessed our endeavors, and many souls were awakened; but the elder soon forbid us holding any such meetings; but we viewed the forlorn state of our colored brethren, and that they were destitute of a place of worship. They were considered as a nuisance.[11]

This story was a repetition of earlier Baptist experiences in Georgia as well as the experiences of other black Methodists in New York (the African Methodist Episcopal Zion church) and in Delaware (the Union church of Africans). Black Christians faced a dilemma. On the one hand, many whites, especially religious leaders, insisted that they remain members of white-controlled churches. But in so doing they were regarded "as a nuisance." Though some blacks remained, others followed leaders such as Andrew Bryan and Richard Allen to form racially separate congregations. In these settings the worshipers had greater freedom in worship, governance, leadership, and could express themselves more forcefully against slavery. Soon various congregations united forces and formed national or regional denominations or conventions: the Union church of Africans in 1813; the African Methodist Episcopal church in 1816; the African Methodist Episcopal Zion church in 1821; the Providence Baptist Association in 1834; The Wood River Association (or Colored Baptist Association and Friends of Humanity) in 1839; and the American Baptist Missionary Convention in 1840.

Hitherto, I mainly have treated by implication evangelistic activities of the independent black congregations and churches in reference to prayer meetings or informal sharings of the gospel. Actually, these groups made systematic efforts to bring others to a knowledge of Christ by supporting ministers in their revival and church-building efforts in other places. It must be understood that evangelism represented the very heart of Christian responsibility for many black Christians, especially Methodists and Baptists. Even as they entered the nineteenth century, independent black churches had not forsaken the strong evangelical thrust that had characterized the earlier black and white evangelistic activists. Clarence E. Walker provides a description of how the evangelical viewed his or her religion.

> For Methodists, religion was more than a ritualistic exercise. They believed that conversation brought the converted into close association with God. Once this was accomplished, it was the duty of the saved to bring God's word to the unredeemed. Operating on these assumptions, the clergy and laity of the A.M.E. Church believed it was their duty to bring the message of God's love and the promise of salvation to America's poor, disadvantaged, and sinful blacks. These ideas provided eighteenth- and nineteenth-century black Methodists with a common belief system that enabled them to connect the temporal and spiritual lives to the civil order.[12]

Of course, Walker focuses upon the Methodists and thus speaks with limited language. The above description is appropriate to all black evangelicals in the nineteenth century—the Methodists, Baptists, and often Presbyterians.

The greatest period for the expansion of basically northern-based, independent black churches was during the final days and after the conclusion of the Civil War in 1865. It was then that these conventions and denominations found the opportunity to enlarge their fellowship by evangelizing unchurched, Southern, ex-slave blacks and by uniting with the "invisible" or secret black churches unmonitored by white slaveholders. For example, during the antebellum years the A.M.E. church's activity in the South was confined mainly to New Orleans and Charleston, South Carolina.[13] There were efforts in non-Southern areas, however, from the very inception of the A.M E. Zion church. These Christians took an active interest in evangelization and missions with much of this earlier thrust from Zion women. For example, the Daughters of Conference, organized in 1821, raised large sums of money to aid missionary ministers as they traveled and established new churches. Mary Roberts, a member of the parent A.M.E. Zion congregation in New York City, the Mother Zion Church, was elected first president of the Daughters of Conference and served enthusiastically and vigorously for more than four decades until she was called to glory. Other prominent leaders in the movement to garner support for education and missions include Eliza Ann Gardner, Sarah J. Eato, and Ellen Stevens.[14]

The African Methodist Episcopal church also participated vigorously in evangelism on the home front. L.L. Berry dates the official beginning of organized missions as 1844 and centered around the activities of William Paul Quinn. Actually, Quinn began evangelizing as early as 1832, but his official appointment as a missionary came in 1844 when the Parent Home and Foreign Missionary Society of the A.M.E. church commissioned him as its first missionary.[15] Berry gives an account of the influence that Quinn exerted upon the 1844 General Conference of the church:

> When Rev. Quinn made his report to the 1844 General Conference, he had covered an area of more than three hundred miles. He had established forty-seven churches with a combined membership of two thousand, had seven traveling preachers and twenty-seven local preachers. He had organized fifty Sunday Schools with two hundred teachers and two thousand scholars and forty temperance societies, and had held seventeen camp meetings.[16]

Nor were these early evangelistic endeavors limited to the black Methodists, says James M. Washington in *Frustrated Fellowship*. He analyzes the activities of early Baptist conventions in the Midwest during the 1830s and 1840s. Among those efforts are missionary attempts of these black Baptists to draw others into the fellowship. The Providence Baptist Association and the Union Association centered in Ohio, the Wood River Association based in Illinois, and the American Baptist Missionary Convention organized in New York City, all supported missionaries and encouraged the establishment of new churches.[17] Washington illustrates the vigor of the Wood River Association that was organized in 1839.

> Between 1839 and 1862 the Wood River Association grew from five to ten churches plus four mission churches as far away as Racine, Wisconsin, and Leavenworth, Kansas. Starting with sixty-four members in 1839, it had more than four hundred in 1862, a remarkable record considering the slow growth of the black community in Illinois and farther west. The Association's camp meetings, held in various parts of the state, became legendary, largely because of great preaching and singing. By inviting noted preachers from such places as St. Louis and Cincinnati, Wood River spread its influences far beyond its boundaries.[18]

But this desire to evangelize other blacks did not end with efforts or visions of securing membership in the United States. Again, we return to the theme of story. Black Christians maintained throughout the nineteenth century that they were God's agents to redeem all the sons and daughters of Africa wherever they were found. It is of great interest, therefore, that in their conventions, associations, and conferences, religious leaders again and again expressed desires to send missionaries to those lands where blacks were non-Christian or non-Protestant, (for example, Africa, Haiti, the West Indies). In some instances the missionary zeal became a partner with colonization efforts. The latter was an attempt principally by certain whites acting through the agency of the American Colonization Society organized in 1816–1817 to repatriate blacks to Africa, specifically in the area that later became the Republic of Liberia. Various motives were at play in this effort of colonization. Some whites and blacks sincerely believed that the caste of race would remain a permanent and insurmountable fixture in the U.S. If blacks hoped ever to be free, it would have to be in a land outside the U.S. In addition, Afro-Americans returning to the homeland would carry Christian civilization to that "backward," "benighted" land and so help it to rise above its "savagery" and become a civilized land. On the other hand, many blacks and some sympathetic whites condemned the colonization movement, noting the convenience to the slaveholder of having all free blacks removed from the country. Escaped slaves would have no communities to which they could flee and secure refuge. Nor would the slaveholders have to contend with the antislavery behavior of the free blacks. Finally, with all free blacks removed, the argument that black slaves set free would not be able to manage on their own could not be concretely refuted by living examples.

Of the independent black churches, the Baptists appear to have the oldest tradition of missionary involvement in Africa and other foreign lands. Leroy Fitts states that the foreign mission movement predated the domestic or home missions movement.[19] He bases this claim upon the traditional rendering of history by black Baptists. According to this account, David George and George Liele would represent the first missionaries of the black Baptist church (to Sierra Leone and Jamaica respectively). It is true that sometime between 1773 and 1775 the first recorded separate black church in the U.S. emerged under the leadership of a white, Palmer; and two blacks, George and Liele. During the British invasion this church was disorganized and then reconstituted in 1793 in Augusta, Georgia. Called the First African Baptist Church, it was located only twelve miles from the original South Carolina site. In the meantime David George and some members moved first to Nova Scotia, Canada. Later some of that party relocated in Sierra Leone where they reputedly established the first Baptist church on the continent. Likewise, George Liele, because of the pro-British sympathy of his military master, was moved to Savannah and later to Jamaica, West Indies. Having been emancipated, Liele worked tirelessly to establish a Baptist presence on the island—an effort crowned with success.[20]

In the sense that these two men went abroad spreading the faith, they must indeed be labeled missionaries. But such an appellation is dubious if we define missionary as someone sent and supported by a church, conference, association, or other agency.

We face a similar dilemma when we view the ministries

of Lott Carey and Colin Teague. With the assistance of white deacon William Crane, the two black Baptists organized the Richmond African Baptist Missionary Society in 1815, one year following the establishment of the first denomination of American Baptists (usually referred to as the Triennial Convention). Carey and Teague sailed for Africa in 1821 under the auspices of the Triennial Convention and the American Colonization Society and supported in part by the Richmond Society. These Baptists certainly set out to spread the gospel in Africa; but along with other free and ex-slave blacks they were permanently relocating to West Africa, specifically Liberia, as colonists. I suppose it would be correct, given all the above factors, to label them as missionary-colonists.[21]

Daniel Coker, an American Methodist Episcopal, actually preceded the black Baptists by one year when he journeyed in 1820 to Sierra Leone, the British colony for repatriated Africans also on Africa's West Coast.[22] Other A.M.E. missionaries (probably colonists, too) journeyed to Liberia in 1822 and to Haiti as early as 1824. In 1840 the A.M.E. church established a conference in Canada.[23] As early as 1829 there was an attempt to connect black Methodist churches in Upper Canada with the A.M.E.Z. church. During the 1850s, with the passage of the Fugitive Slave Law and the historic Dred Scott decision handed down by the U.S. Supreme Court, the freedom of all escaped slaves was in jeopardy. An escaped slave living in free territory had no guarantee that a slaveholder could not legally demand that he or she be returned to slavery. Indeed, many blacks born free could be unjustly accused of being runaways and forced into slavery. It is in this climate that the A.M.E.Z. agreed that its Canadian siblings in the faith should be free to organize their own separate general conference.[24]

In summation, except for occasional missionaries sent to the Caribbean area or the establishment of Methodist conferences and Baptist associations in Canada, most of the foreign mission endeavors by Christians in the independent black churches preceding the Civil War were in the style of Carey and Teague: missionary colonization in Africa, usually Liberia. To be sure, the black churches, such as the American Baptist Missionary Convention, often voiced sincere interest in and devoted attention to evangelizing foreign lands with large black populations, especially Africa. But concerns on the domestic front such as lack of human and financial resources, caring for the needs of the domestic church, and the fight against slavery, absorbed the overwhelming bulk of their time and energies. It was not until after the Civil War that the black churches embarked upon a more deliberate, consistent, systematic course in foreign (and especially African) missions.

We have stated that the combination of missionary endeavors with African colonization characterized some of the evangelistic outreach (particularly in reference to foreign missions) of black Christians during the pre-Civil War years. It should be emphasized, however, that most blacks—including black church leaders—at best distrusted the efforts of the American Colonization Society and usually campaigned actively against them. Granted, black leaders, both church and nonchurch, advocated that individual blacks should be free to emigrate should they so desire. But they made a great distinction between the voluntary emigration of individuals and their families seeking to improve their lot in the world (even through the instrumentality of the American Colonization Society) and the systematic efforts of white proponents of colonization to organize massive transferrals of Afro-Americans back to the motherland. Again, black religious leaders understood the colonization scheme as a plan to rid the country of free blacks and thus strengthen the system of slavery. Even the claim by black and white religious persons, such as Lott Carey, that the repatriation of blacks in Africa would support the development of a Christian civilization, sounded unconvincing to many black church people. Though they firmly believed that the implantation of a Christian civilization in Africa would produce both spiritual and material advancement for the entire African race (and that such was the will of God), they did not envision most of the freed slaves as being the most effective communicators of such a blessing. A.M.E. Bishop Richard Allen, an antislavery spokesperson and opponent of African colonization, made the point that black slaves were deliberately denied education and many other refinements of life by the slaveholder so that he or she might be in a better position to keep them in subjugation. The colonizationists hoped to convince slaveholders to free the slaves on the condition that they emigrate to Africa. With so many black slaves ignorant and lacking a firm grasp of Christian fundamentals, how could one expect that they would spread Christian civilization? According to Allen:

> We are an unlettered people, brought up in ignorance, not one in a hundred can read or write, not one in a thousand has a liberal education; is there any fitness for such to be sent into a far country, among heathens, to convert or civilize them, when they themselves are neither civilized or Christianized? See the great bulk of the poor, ignorant Africans in this country, exposed to every temptation before them: all for the want of their morals being refined by education and proper attendance paid unto them by their owners, or those who had the charge of them. . . . Is there any fitness for such a people to be colonized in a far country to be their own rulers?[25]

Black church spokespersons not only criticized the missionary-colonization efforts and motivations of white Christians, they also on occasion questioned the very validity or appropriateness of general foreign mission activities by whites in all non-Christian lands. To reiterate, they believed in evangelism and saw it as a powerful tool to uplift people spiritually and materially. However, they could not forget the harsh treatment that the overwhelming majority of free and enslaved Afro-Americans received at the hands of many white Christians or that the latter refused to counteract by the application of Christian charity. So, how could whites expect the world to take them seriously as missionaries of the Christian gospel if they did not practice it at home among their own Christian family? Secondly, where is the sense in traveling over the world proclaiming the message of salvation to "heathens" in faraway lands when there was a multitude of unconverted blacks in their own midst? Black Christians were challenging the very legitimacy of white Christians' understanding of the message of Christ and the obligation it entailed for those who claimed to receive it.

David Walker, a natural free black of North Carolina, moved to Boston and began to protest slavery. In his *Appeal in Four Articles,* published in 1829, he called for the enslaved to rise up in violent defiance of their wretched condition and to demand the freedom given to them by God. A decade or so later Henry Highland Garnet, a prominent Presbyterian minister and abolitionist, would circulate Walker's *Appeal* with his own *Address to the Slaves,* thus indicating the profound esteem in which he regarded the earlier tract. Even if one claims that some of Walker's sentiments are somewhat outside the mainstream of antebellum black religious thought, his views are generally reflective of the concerns of practically all black church leaders and specifically reflective of some.

Walker's *Appeal* contains some very interesting comments concerning the problem of evil, the history and intrinsic nature of whites, and the suitability of white American Christians to engage in foreign missions. Like other black leaders, Walker faced the question of evil specifically as it applied to the black condition in the U.S. Why do black people suffer such grievances, wrongs, and brutality at the hands of white so-called Christians? Interestingly, he maintained that the only reason acceptable was the mere fact that whites held blacks in slavery to enrich themselves and the nation. Of course this situation would not last forever. If whites did not repent, then God would soon unleash his judgment upon the wicked nation—which could be viewed as a prophecy of the Civil War that commenced about thirty years later.[26]

Walker believed that the contemporary barbarity of white Americans was perfectly consistent with the entire history of the white race. Wherever we view them in history, in ancient times or in more recent centuries, they behave in a manner clearly, unequivocally more wicked than Africans and Asians, Walker stated.

> The whites have always been an unjust, jealous, unmerciful, avaricious and bloodthirsty set of beings, always seek-

> ing after power and authority . . . I find, we view them all
> over Europe, together with what was scattered about in
> Asia and Africa, as heathens, and we see them acting more
> like devils than accountable men. . . .[27]

Even the introduction of Christianity among them had
not reduced their zeal for oppression. Indeed, it seemed
to have manifested it! It was after their "acceptance" of
Christianity that whites engaged in the slave trade with
its brutal, horrifying treatment of men, women, and children. The American system of chattel slavery was the
worst form of bondage that the world had ever wit-
nessed—far more cruel than the enslavement of the Hebrews in Egypt! If God would grant them greater
knowledge, declared Walker, they would seek to overthrow the Almighty himself.[28] These observations led
Walker to question the very structure of human nature
among whites.

> I therefore, in the name and fear of the Lord God
> of heaven and of earth, divested of prejudice either on
> the side of my color or that of the whites, advance my
> suspicion of them, whether they are as good by nature
> as we are or not. Their actions, since they were known
> as a people, have been the reverse, I do indeed suspect
> them [of having an inferior human nature of goodness],
> but this, as I before observed, is shut up with the Lord,
> we cannot exactly tell it will be loved in succeeding gen-
> erations. . . .[29]

This concern about the history, behavior, and human
nature of whites had particular relevance to the black
Christians' understanding of their capacity to engage ef-
fectively in foreign missions. Indeed, Walker claimed that
the most reliable instruments for evangelizing in the
world were Afro-Americans who at that time suffered at
the hands of whites.

> It is my solemn belief, that if ever the world become
> Christianized, (which must certainly take place before
> long), it will be through the means, under God, of the
> Blacks, who are now held in wretchedness, and degrada-
> tion by the white Christians of the world. . . .[30]

There was no reason for white American Christians to embark upon foreign mission ventures without first having reconciled themselves with and done justice to blacks.

> ... they must learn to do justice at home, before they go into distant lands, to display their charity, Christianity, and benevolence; when they learn to do justice, God will accept their offering (no man may think that I am against Missionaries for I am not, my object is to see justice done at home before we go to convert the heathens).[31]

The extended attention paid to Walker's *Appeal* is meant to demonstrate the significance that evangelism had in the thinking of antebellum black Christians. Even in the writing of this revolutionary, we have the affirmation of evangelism and the confident assurance that its object, the Christian faith, will soon encircle the globe. Second, black people were to convey a crucial role in world evangelism because they best represented the true, holistic understanding of the Christian gospel. The second point is a reflection of the Afro-American Christian story: blacks, kidnapped and sold from their natural lands, transported like beasts, and treated as animals in the land of freedom, had a special place in the plans of God. God was fashioning them, despite and even through the system of slavery, to teach the world the true meaning of the Christian faith.

Third, though not made clear in the above citation, the *Appeal* reflects general black Christian sentiment that Protestantism is the true religion and that Catholicism is a "plague." In another place, Walker extols the nation of Haiti as "the glory of the blacks and terror of tyrants." Blacks felt particularly proud of this nation of people that successfully rebelled against their white French colonists and slaveholders and established an independent nation around the turn of the nineteenth century. It was a reflection of the "manhood" of blacks and a living example that African people could govern themselves. But black Christians occasionally supported missionaries to Haiti to remove the "scourge" of Catholicism and to lift the people to the heights of freedom, democracy, and Christianity. Practically all black Christian leaders (and most of them were Protestants) agreed with these sentiments of Walker.

> I am sorry to say it [Haiti] is plagued with the scourge of nations, the Catholic religion; but I hope and pray God that she may yet rid herself of it, and adapt in its stead the Protestant faith. . . .[32]

In sum, Walker's *Appeal,* authored by a layman, accurately reflects the general tenor of the black church's views of evangelism even though it is a treatise supporting the violent overthrow of slavery.

Finally, we should bear in mind that the black independent denominations and independent churches abhorred American slavery. They made active protest against the system by a number of means which included denominational disciplines and bylaws stating that they regarded slavery as an evil to be eradicated as soon as possible, providing and supporting spokespersons who labored against the perpetuation of the practice, and by allowing their church buildings and the homes of their parishioners to be used as havens for escaped slaves. This antislavery stance led the early black Christians to draw a clear line of demarcation between the religion of the majority of white Christians and that which they held to be the true gospel of Christ. Frederick Douglass, the abolitionist and outspoken advocate of racial justice, made it very clear in his 1845 autobiography that his devastating critique of religion was directed toward what he considered to be the hypocritical, slaveholding Christianity—not the religion preached by Christ.

> I love the pure, peaceable, and impartial Christianity of Christ; I therefore hate the corrupt, slave-holding, women-whipping, cradle-plundering, partial and hypocritical Christianity of the land. . . .[33]

It must be remembered that these early black Christians were largely evangelical in outlook. They saw the slave system as prohibiting genuine access to Christianity for the enslaved. As the previous reference to Richard Allen states, slavery kept the masses of people in spiritual blindness, as "heathens" outside the ark of salvation.

Therefore, much abolitionist sentiment was influenced by and premised upon the need to abolish slavery so that the people might hear the genuine gospel in its totality. It was this viewpoint that Henry H. Garnet, the abolitionist and Presbyterian leader, sought to convey in his 1843 *Address to the Slaves.*

> [God] requires you to love him supremely, and your neighbor as yourself, to keep the Sabbath day holy, to search the Scriptures, and bring up your children with respect for his laws, and to worship no other God but him. But slavery sets all of these at naught, and hurls defiance in the face of Jehovah. . . .[34]

Garnet made the point that one could not serve two masters. Those in bondage had to decide whose slaves they were—Christ's or the white slaveholder's. He continued:

> The forlorn condition in which you are placed does not destroy your moral obligation to God. . . . God will not receive slavery, nor ignorance, nor any other state of mind, for love and obedience to him. Your condition does not absolve you from your moral obligation. . . .[35]

Therefore, one had no choice but to rebel against the slaveholder.

It would be incorrect to state that the black religious abolitionism was merely a form of evangelism. But I do wish to emphasize that there was an evangelistic significance to abolitionism. Thus, the story shows that the black church actively engaged in evangelistic activities during the pre-Civil War years by various means, which included supporting missionary personnel, founding new churches, engaging in foreign missions, and spearheading the abolitionist movement.

CHAPTER 3

Recovery of the Story: Evangelism and Slave Religion

*I*n this chapter I wish to devote special attention to two areas of evangelism as it was operative in the lives of those black people who were held in bondage and in the period during and following the Civil War. It is very gratifying to read and report about those blacks who were born free, emancipated, or who escaped. The story of their devotion to the gospel of Christ and ever-abiding commitments to their parents, siblings, children, and friends still held in bondage strikes chords of joy in those of us still committed to social justice. It is even more delightful that they expressed these sentiments by words and actions through the black- and even some white-controlled churches. These individuals and groups have our undying devotion.

But the real heroes and heroines, without detracting from the above statements, are those men, women, and children who endured the barren, brutal system of chattel slavery. Given all the adversities they experienced and met, notwithstanding the bondage-derived scars that still plague Afro-Americans even today, it is a wonder that blacks emerged from such a condition as whole, hopeful, healthy, and confident as they did. Increasingly it is becoming apparent to both "secular" and "religious" historians and other scholars that the slaves' faith in Christ contributed immeasurably—probably indispensably—to their wholeness and health. In Christ they found not only hope in a blessed future or afterlife that would render their present sufferings inconsequential, but they also discovered strength and joy in the present days and hours. They found a transcendental meaning of life that would sooner or later make itself known in judgment upon oppression.

As we embark upon a study of their religion, it must be understood that Afro-Americans had a solid, holistic understanding of the faith about which they spoke. Due to the magnificent research by scholars such as Albert Raboteau and Lawrence Levine,[1] we have the opportunity to witness the power of the faith and its effect in the lives of people relegated to the bottom of societies. In their experiences, joys, sufferings, and hopes we catch a profound glimpse of Christianity as it was encountered by similar people nearly two thousand years ago when the faith was in its golden age.

Before we proceed, it is necessary to note that the most complete picture of slave religion we have is that of their worship beyond the observation of whites. Often this series of worship, prayers, devotion, and so forth of slaves is termed "invisible institution" because it was unseen by whites. Scholars contend that it is through the invisible institution that we discover the essence of black religious experience during slavery. The slaves would "steal away" to secluded places so that they might worship God freely and undisturbed by whites. Meeting places varied but included cabins and secret places on the farm.

The edited work, *God Struck Me Dead* is a collection of experiences of slaves as recorded in the twentieth century when these persons were advanced in age. They crystallize the Christian slaves' encounters with God and how those encounters motivated them to share the good news with others. Note one account that records a portion of an individual's encounter with God. He had "wanted to be converted" and responded to an invitation by a minister to attend a revival.

> I went on to church, and the brothers and sisters prayed around me. Then, like a flash, the power of God struck me.

> It seemed like something struck me in the top of my head and then went on out through my toes of my feet. I jumped, or rather fell back against the back of the seat. I lay on the floor of the church. A voice said to me, "you are no longer a sinner. Go and tell the world what I have done for you. If you are ashamed of me, I will be ashamed of you before my father. . . ."[2]

His spiritual experiences lasted until dawn. The narrator of the account testified to a clear change in his character and life. He now discovered that he had a deep love for everybody and all of God's creation. Furthermore, he testified that since conversion he no longer felt fear toward anyone. This person's life was now characterized by the chief Christian virtue.

> I can't tell you what religion is, only that it is love. If I do anybody wrong I feel grieved, get down on my knees, and ask for forgiveness from them. When the (Spirit) struck me it seemed to hit me in the top of my head and go out through my feet. There is no such thing as getting religion, for it is love and a gift from God.[3]

Of course, the conversion and other spiritual experiences of the slaves varied as they do with other people in other times and places. Some conversion experiences tended to involve powerful emotions, visions, and voices. Others were quieter or were accompanied by less visible manifestations. But the above-cited account is representative of a number of significant points as they relate to evangelism. First, most of the evangelism of blacks occurred within the context of the slave community. In part this is because the slaves trusted their own religious leaders more than they trusted white missionaries. In many instances the white preacher in the nineteenth century had accommodated his message to the system of slavery and the approval of slaveholders, unlike most of the earliest eighteenth-century antislavery evangelical ministers. The existence of the invisible institution permitted Afro-Americans to reject the "religion of the masters" and interpret the faith in a manner that suited their needs. Lawrence W. Levine writes:

> Slaves simply refused to be uncritical recipients of a religion defined and controlled by white intermediaries and interpreters. No matter how respectfully and attentively they might listen to the white preachers, no matter how well they might sing the traditional hymns, it was their own preachers and their own songs which stirred them the most.[4]

Even well into the post-Civil War period the black community retained a high regard for the black preacher.

Second, we observe from the previous account that evangelism in the community was not only informal but also very often (if not usually) occurred with or without the slave preacher. In other words, the Christian community as a whole assumed the responsibility of spreading the faith to the sinner. The above account exemplifies the use of the "mourner's bench." Note that the Christian community as a whole ("the brothers and sisters")—not simply the preacher—prayed for the seeker of salvation. The conversion evangelical religion can become overly individualistic or privatistic. The mourner's bench connected the seeker with the rest of the community. The seeker needed the support of the community and its prayers.

Based upon these observations, we might term the Christian theology of the slave community as a "family theology." Parents and children, brothers and sisters, and husbands and wives who had been torn from one another at the whim of the economic advantage of the slaveholder found a new family in the solidarity of the black community. If we examine the slave songs we will note the absence of any reference to whites.

> The slave's positive reference group was composed entirely of his own peers: his mother, father, sister, brother, uncles, aunts, preacher, fellow "sinners" and "mourners" of whom he sang endlessly, to whom he sent messages via the dying, and with whom he was reunited joyfully in the next world.[5]

Very often Christianity (as defined by Afro-Americans) became almost synonymous with the slave community.

The pervasive view was Christian and was shared even by those who were not really members of the church fellowship. It often was difficult to exist within the slave community without being pulled into the orbit of faith. This is not to suggest that Christians attempted to force sinners to convert. But the very power of God made manifest through the earnest and sincere lifestyle of the faithful attracted the unconverted both to the judgment and the grace of the gospel message.[6]

It often has been noted by scholars that the religions of Africa do not lend themselves to a view of the world where persons, things, activities, and events are neatly separated into a religious and a secular sphere. All of life is seen as falling within the purview of the sacred. This is true. One could argue that Afro-American Christianity retained elements of the African in this regard. This is also true. But the same holistic perspective regarding the sacredness of life is found wherever religion operates. The truly faithful and dedicated do not place parameters upon the activity of the Divine in life affairs. This principle applies particularly when people have little in the way of leisure time and material possessions, where they find themselves in a constant struggle to survive and affirm their humanity. The Afro-American slaves did not require formal meetings whether they took place in the view of the slaveholders or whether they were unseen by them. Christ said where two or three were gathered in his name he would be there in the midst of them. The sweet irony of the enslaved blacks' experiences is that the slaveholders forced them to gather for work. But the Christ within them often changed the agenda of the gathering. Spontaneously, the work place became a church meeting.

Again, Afro-American slaves understood well the message of the Gospel of John: true worship is not dependent upon a given place—no matter how sacredly it is perceived—but a state of mind centered on Christ.

One former slave remembered how religious enthusiasm could begin simply with a group of slaves sitting in front of their cabins after supper on a summer evening. Someone might start humming an old hymn; the humming would spread from house to house and would be transferred into song. . . .[7]

It was often in this type of setting that sinners would be converted without organized, systematic mission programs, without the necessary presence of a minister or missionary, and without the context of a formal worship service. The community at large was a family of brothers and sisters sharing common sufferings and pains and similar joys and triumphs. The power of God and the love and solidarity of this extended, communal family were the foundations for slave evangelism.

We have seen previously that the independent black church understood Christianity as antithetical to the system of slavery. For these black Christians faith entailed both a personal and social dimension. Christ did in fact renew the sinner's life—granting him or her personal salvation, joy, and peace in this world and eternal life in the next. From a social perspective these Christians believed that God required them to become actively engaged in the civil order to insure justice, including the eradication of slavery.

The previous quote relating to conversion experience illustrates that the enslaved black church shared an understanding of the faith as bringing personal salvation. Indeed, this aspect never really is doubted. The question remains, did Afro-American slaves see religion as encompassing the social aspect as well as the personal? Specifically, did they envision God as acting in history to obliterate slavery? If so, what was the relationship between the personal and social dimension of the faith?

It would be grossly inaccurate to contend that Christian slaves propagated the faith solely in order to bring physical emancipation to their fellow slaves. It seems abundantly clear from any serious study of the spirituals as well as the narratives of slaves and ex-slaves that the primary concern of Christian slaves was salvation. To interpret the accounts recorded in *God Struck Me Dead*, for example, as slaves being overly concerned with liberation as a motivation for their search for and response to God is to do serious damage to the integrity of these Afro-American forebears and black Christianity in particular.

But it also would be absolutely correct to maintain that most slaves saw slavery as abhorrently inconsistent with true Christianity. They prayed and sang, subtly and sometimes in songs with double meaning, about physical liberation from chattel bondage. Based upon the sum of their songs, prayers, and accounts that have come down to us, we may confidently declare that they understood God to be on the side of freedom; that they, like David Walker, expected a divine reckoning in human affairs setting them free spiritually and physically. Like their Northern siblings in the faith, they understood Christianity as a holistic religion encompassing both the spiritual and the temporal.

It is not surprising, therefore, that the slave preacher often was the leading contact person in the system of aiding slaves to escape, hiding them en route to freedom, and securing final accommodations for living once their journey to freedom was completed. Not only was the minister engaged in this system of "Underground Railroad," but also once he and the faithful community were unobserved by whites he would often speak clearly and boldly of God's liberating activity in history, the present, and the future. No wonder the preacher would remain a popular and highly admired figure in the black community well after the Emancipation.

But the minister, ordained or unordained by white-recognized church bodies or representatives, important though he was, did not dominate the religious community of the enslaved. With the slave community we have a set of affairs closely akin to many if not most early Christian communities in the apostolic and subapostolic age: genuine communalism and mutual sharing based upon the understanding of the entire community as a Christian extended family of brothers and sisters, mothers and fathers, and elders and youth. Thus the personal and social dimensions of the faith reflected and acted out by the minister (for example, in antislavery activities) characterized the belief system and behavior of the general Christian community.

In this respect this early Christian slave community left a legacy that could well be a source of guidance for those of us concerned about social action today. Namely, their strivings and yearnings for physical and social deliverance from the persons and systems of oppression were deeply rooted in their quest and apprehension of the Christian faith. In other words, their quest for social salvation was established upon the faithful assurance that they had been spiritually liberated. The slaves' overarching concern was achieving or receiving God's grace in Christ that delivered them from the bondage of personal sin, while also achieving deliverance from chattel slavery.

In an account of the life of Harriet Tubman, a conductor on the Underground Railroad and a faithful member of the Zion Methodist fellowship, one sees a very significant illustration of the above.[8] Tubman was subjected to the mean, brutal treatment of a Maryland slaveholder. Her oppression was so great that she called upon the Lord to either change him or to kill him. Shortly after this prayer the slaveholder died. After her own escape from slavery, this courageous, future liberator would personally return to slave territory time and again and lead numerous slaves to their freedom. The curious and perhaps surprising thing about this victim of numerous acts and enduring conditions of oppression was her reaction to the death of the brutal slaveholder. She felt guilty, believing that her prayer for his demise had been answered.

Tubman and her fellow Christian slaves knew that something was seriously wrong with the human condition. They refused to let the misfortunes and brutality they experienced under the system of chattel slavery overshadow the fundamental truth that all human beings, both the oppressors and the oppressed, are cursed with the awful reality of sinfulness. It is true, as Raboteau[9] and other authors so clearly demonstrate, that their system of ethics did not always correspond exactly with what the slaveholders and the slaveholders' preferred preachers desired or expected, particularly as applied to their day-to-day survival and maintenance of group cohesion and integrity. But neither did they pass the spiritual "buck." They owned their sinfulness and unworthiness and in return secured God's grace that gave them new life.

It is upon the reception of a new life, liberated from spiritual bondage, that Christian slaves and former slaves could then enter into a more authentic quest for political liberation. Wimberly and Wimberly discuss this phenomenon in relation to Harriet Tubman.

> It was out of this spiritual freedom that she decided to move toward her material, economic, and social freedom. It was after her experience of God's forgiveness that she was assured God would lead her and others in her race to freedom. It was at the moment of her spiritual liberation that she realized that social liberation from slavery was possible.[10]

In other words, the acknowledgment of her own personal need for salvation did not lead her to adopt an otherworldly approach to the faith that would have rendered her inactive in the quest for political freedom. Quite the contrary—personal and social salvation for her went hand in hand.

> Freedom from slavery and salvation from personal sin are closely related themes in the slave material. They are intimately connected. As indicated in the life of Harriet Tubman, the desire for social deliverance burned deep in her breast along with the desire for personal salvation. Personal and social salvation mutually influenced each other in the slave tradition.[11]

The interrelatedness between personal and social salvation also was seen in the conversion stories of other freedom fighters born in slavery, such as James W. C. Pennington and Sojourner Truth.[12]

Finally, we need to say something relative to the self-concept of Afro-Americans held in bondage. The independent black church people looked upon themselves as a special, chosen people, believing that they were far better models of the meaning of the Christian gospel than their white counterparts. It must be noted that Christianity is by nature a missionary type of religion. Christians believe that God has called them to bear witness of the gospel throughout the world. The idea of Christian mission becomes intimately and sometimes almost inextricably linked with a nation, culture, or racial group. Sometimes this identification of religious mission assumes a secondary role to a nation's or group's "secular'" or patriotic concerns. When this occurs, a nation or group views itself as a chosen people to spread their culture throughout the world, convinced that their way of life is superior to all others and ordained by God. In American history whites have subscribed to this manner of thinking in pursuit of their "manifest destiny" and "the white man's burden."

In a previous section, we have discussed the role of story among free Afro-American Christians, their confident belief that the destiny of all descendants of Africa is one, and that black American Christians had a special role under God in leading their racial kin to that destiny. Furthermore, the African race, once fully regenerated under the influence of the gospel and democracy, then would teach the world the authentic meaning of these blessings. If free blacks developed such a self-concept in the context of white prejudice, segregation, and discrimination in the North, it is not surprising that Southern blacks, suffering under the bonds of chattel slavery, would develop a similar concept based upon their experiences with the slaveholder.

This idea of chosen people appears in the tradition of both free and enslaved blacks because both derived their theologies from the Bible.[13] It is of great significance to note that the ideas, themes, and beliefs that permeated black spirituals, prayers, and other aspects of worship had their foundation in the Scriptures. Reading the Bible or any other literature was outlawed in the South, particularly after Nat Turner led the slave revolt around 1830. Yet certain individuals by one means or another gained access to the skill of reading and passed the rewards of such an accomplishment to their fellow slaves. Of course songs, prayers, preaching, and so forth, were effective repositories and transports for biblical truths even if the communicator was unable to read.

According to Lawrence Levine, "The most persistent single image the slave songs contain is that of the chosen people."[14] They envisioned themselves as a community called out by God, over whom God watched, and for whom God would intervene in judgment. This community, as noted earlier, did not include whites. As a matter of fact, many Afro-American slaves refused to believe that whites would live in heaven. Hell was the appropriate place for a people who had been so cruel. Though the slaves did not identify with whites, they did look upon biblical heroes and heroines as intimate friends, even as relatives, calling them brothers and sisters. Many scholars have noted that the slaves had a strong attachment to the Old Testament with its emphasis upon God's acting in this life to free, protect, and guide the ancient Hebrews through various adversities. Unsurprisingly, the American slaves identified with their Hebrew counterparts in Pharaoh's Egypt and with individuals such as Daniel (in the lion's den) faced with similar circumstances. When they turned attention upon the New Testament, much of it focused upon the love, suffering, death, and resurrection of Jesus, the apocalyptic coming of God's judgment to a wicked world, and promises of afterlife in heaven noted in passages located in the book of Revelation.

What is the significance of the above discussion for our look at evangelism? It is this: The Christian religion was an intimate, serious experience for the enslaved faithful. They did not simply accept religion as passed to them by whites. Instead, they fashioned the faith to suit their own needs without distorting its basic doctrinal content. Thus, they sought to share with one another—and occasionally whites—not white propaganda but the reality of Christ's love. As a result, they, under God, created one of the most powerful means of evangelism that has survived in many places well into the twentieth century: a committed, Christ-centered community that almost unconsciously reaches out to others automatically, bringing them into God's church.

Black Evangelism: The Civil War and the Aftermath, 1860–1920

It is during this period that we come to perhaps the most fascinating era in the black church regarding institutional evangelism. Both free and enslaved black Christians had prayed and dreamed of the day when God would act in history to free his chosen from chattel bondage. There were many whites who regarded the war as a struggle to hold together the union of the States. But blacks from the beginning dreamed, and as the war progressed became convinced, that God was acting through this conflict to redeem the slaves. The year 1863, when President Abraham Lincoln signed the Emancipation Proclamation, became the year of great significance. This executive order signed as an emergency war measure only promised freedom to enslaved blacks in states in active rebellion against the U.S. government. Yet somehow people, black and white, knew that the war now had become a conflict to rid the country of slavery.

As the fighting progressed, the U.S. government became more receptive to the idea of black soldiers serving in the federal forces because the Southern white rebels proved more of a successful challenge to the white Union soldiers than had been expected. With the Emancipation Proclamation, black leaders who had been reluctant to approve the recruitment of Afro-Americans for service in the U.S. forces altered their position and supported the cause. As free black and white soldiers marched into the South, Southern black and white missionizing enslaved blacks either marched with or shortly followed them.

Black Baptists and Methodists were among the soldiers in the Lord's Army. James M. Washington observed that as early as August 1863 the American Baptist Missionary Convention—a black group organized in 1840 in New York City—received permission from the U.S. president to follow the Union soldiers and to evangelize their brothers and sisters.[15] The scholarly, dedicated leader in the A.M.E. church, Daniel Alexander Payne, gave a poignant and theologically significant account of his experiences when he returned to his home city of Charleston, South Carolina, during the final months of the Civil War.[16] He speaks of his interdenominational contacts and activities there in the city. He was pleased to note the presence of black schools where the students were under the instruction of pro-freedom, Northern white teachers; and he spoke with pride of the fact that black U.S. troops stood guard in the city.

Payne provided an account of his days there that revealed the destructive aspect of the war but also mirrored the apprehension of many black and white Christians regarding the religious significance of the conflict.

> Destruction marks every square through which we passed. . . . All showed the devastating hand of war, and the hot indignation of that God who, when he stretches out his arm against the oppressor, never draws it back till every fetter is broken and every slave is free. . . .[17]

Payne experienced what he and many other black Christians, slave and free, had dreamed of and prayed for for years. God had finally intervened in human affairs on behalf of "a helpless race" to lift them to freedom and a higher order of civilization.

> . . .[My] emotions overwhelmed me, and expressed themselves in tears of gratitude, thanksgiving, and love to that God who had wrought such a marvelous change in the condition of a helpless race. There and then I realized the fulfillment of the promises which God the Father of all the families of the earth had made to me in 1835. . . . I believed what I beheld was a prophecy of the future, the New England ideas, sentiments, and principles will ultimately rule the entire South. . . .[18]

Some years ago a very perceptive critic in his book *Is God a White Racist?* dared the propagators and defenders of black theology to provide concrete proof of their claim that God acts in history to free those oppressed.[19] More specifically, he challenged them to prove by concrete example that God is not a racist, that he is on the side of blacks in their struggle for freedom. A theologically correct response is that Christianity is a matter of faith that does not always lend itself to rational analysis and verification. A more historically accurate response is that the community of black Christians (and many whites) have affirmed that the Union victory in the Civil War was God's victory over slavery. This community said that the emancipated American slaves had been taken out of the clutches of avaricious and brutal pharaohs who knew not Joseph, nor had a sufficiently correct idea about the love and general purpose of Joseph's God whom these pharaohs claimed to serve. But let us return to the wartime activities of black missionaries in the South.

The AMEZ, like the black Baptists and the AME, also extended their churches southward to evangelize slaves, incorporate black Christian communities into the denomination, and to establish new churches.[20] Along these lines, Joseph Jackson Clinton, the first appointed bishop for the South, played a major role. Elected at the youthful age of thirty-three, Clinton during these years commissioned five missionaries to evangelize and organize the church in the South. Perhaps the best known and most successful of these men was James Walker Hood, who was later elected a Zion bishop. Hood pioneered the work in the South, operating chiefly in the North Carolina cities of New Bern, Wilmington, Fayetteville, and Charlotte. Indeed, Hood's activities soon extended beyond the realm of strictly ecclesiastical activities. He was quite active in politics during the Reconstruction era, helping to frame a new state constitution and serving as assistant superintendent of education in North Carolina. Along with J. C. Price, whom he inducted into the AME Zion program of black education, he cofounded Livingstone College in Salisbury, North Carolina. It should be emphasized that black Christians refused to take a backseat to their white counterparts in the pursuit of evangelizing their Southern racial siblings. They insisted that the work should be their main responsibility. This viewpoint coincided with their prewar declaration that God would act through them to secure the blessings of Christianity and democratic civilization to all of the descendants of Africa, and ultimately teach the entire world the true meaning of democratic, Christian civilization. Whites, by their support of racism, segregation, and slavery, had rendered themselves unfit for such a glorious but highly responsible role. James Washington analyzed the notion of chosen people that even in the postwar years still dominated the thinking of black Baptists.

> Northern black Baptists, most of them immigrants from the South, especially from Virginia, felt a strong obligation to evangelize among their own brethren. In fact their belief in themselves as a Saving Remnant, manifest before the war, became even more pronounced after the war. Their basic agenda entitled saving freed black Southerners and especially potential young ministers, who in turn would provide personnel that they never had before the war to spread the gospel among blacks in the West Indies and Africa.[21]

Nor did Baptists have a monopoly on such sentiments. Clarence Walker describes the sense of mission that the AME church felt toward Southern blacks.

> A sense of mission set the A.M.E. Church off from other groups of black Christians. The clergy and laity of the church saw themselves as agents of God for the task of elevating the [black] race in America, a task they thought was theirs because they were Methodist and black. . . .[22]

Of course the first sentence of the previous quote is inaccurate with the possible exception that it is meant to describe the AME's self-concept of its mission. The above quote from Washington as well as others from various groups, including the AMEZ, demonstrate that each group and all black Christians envisioned themselves as special instruments of God. Furthermore, the following pages will reveal that Methodists, like Baptists, saw their divine vocation as extending beyond the U.S. to envision other lands where blacks lived, especially Africa.

Preaching, organizing new churches, and incorporating existing Christian slave communities into the institutional denominations, associations, and conventions were not the only means that Northern black missionaries employed to evangelize Southern blacks. As Litwack observes, they, like white missionaries and sometimes in cooperation with them, used education and the construction of schools to expand the Christian fellowship.[23] These

Northern missionaries saw their Southern kin as so degraded by the slave system that they required the teacher as well as the preacher and the soldier. Education and religion went hand in hand; often the minister or missionary and the teacher were the same individual. But even if the individuals involved had different titles, their goals often were the same and usually overlapped. Indeed, many schools and colleges originated black church buildings. Black Christians, North and South, established educational institutions either on their own or in collaboration with white Christians and philanthropists. These schools were permeated with the sense of Christian vocation and the need to evangelize the world, especially the black lands. No wonder there are numerous accounts of men, women, and children who were converted "within the walls of academia" or whatever structure served as a school building. Finally these institutions became significant centers for the selection and training of African missionaries and the converts they encouraged to come to the U.S. for education.

The zeal on behalf of Northern black and white missionaries in the South, however sincere and selfless that zeal might have been, often met with an equal, opposing zeal on behalf of the Southern Christians. This state of affairs occurred primarily when the outsiders sought to disrupt aspects of traditional culture and spirituality in order to refashion them in the mold that they, the Northerners, had become accustomed to. The Northern Christians seemed particularly concerned about what they regarded as an excess of emotion and ecstasy in the worship services. It was a common feature in the worship experience of many ex-slaves to fall, kick, roll, crawl, and squeal.[24] The ex-slave preacher was often described by these Northerners as being ignorant, using incorrect grammar, and speaking and preaching in an incoherent manner. To be sure, many newcomers testified to those traits that they, too, agreed were positive aspects of the ex-slave worship and spiritual life: simplicity, sincerity, earnestness, firm faith, the powerful effects of prayers, the music, and the practical applications of the faith. But it now was time, with the coming of freedom, to strive to match their zeal and sincerity with education and an appreciation for "proper order." In fairness to the newcomers, it must be stressed that they were not strangers to the significant role of emotion in worship. Their goal was not to eliminate all visible expressions of joy and thanksgiving but to eradicate what they saw as excesses. Besides, some local preachers were hypocrites and cheats who were "fleecing the flocks"—their priority was their own material enrichment, not the spiritual advancement of the community of faith.[25]

But one still wonders if the newcomers had not come with certain presuppositions and were too biased in thinking to place them under scrutiny. Is it possible that their religiosity had moved too far in the direction of staidness, with an overemphasis upon proper order and with too little emphasis upon the freedom of the Spirit? For decades abolitionists had railed against the moral degradation being imposed upon blacks under the yoke of slavery, how they were treated as brutes and not accorded sufficient opportunities to embrace the fullness of the gospel. Is it possible that these abolition-minded evangelists did not see a clear truth as expounded by Thomas Wentworth Higginson, that the emotionalism of the slaves made them feel closer to God? As Higginson pointed out, the religion of the slave abrogated much of the moral degradation about which abolitionists had worried.[26] It is quite possible that the newcomers' preconceptions, along with the very different behavior of the slaves and their lack of formal education, blinded them to the reality of the power of God within the ex-slave community and the opportunity the Northern evangelists had to learn from their Southern siblings.

The ex-slaves had practiced their religiosity for decades. God had raised up men who did not necessarily have the ordination or sufficient literary qualifications demanded by white-controlled organizations. Their spontaneous worship services and mourner's bench had been powerful tools of God to bring the wayward and the sinner to God. Religion, they insisted, was not something neatly and intellectually expounded with proper grammar in an orderly gathering. Instead, it was a heartfelt experience that engulfed the whole person and empowered him or her to derive joy and peace even in the midst of profound sadness and turmoil. One wonders if both the white and black Northern missionaries often reminded the ex-slaves of the slaveholder appointed or approved preacher who preached a form of religion with insufficient power. It appears that the Northern missionaries all too often brought with them a form of order and discipline that threatened the liberty in church affairs that the ex-slaves had known. In the slave community, as in the earliest church during the apostolic age, worship and Christian service were responsibilities and privileges of every member. It seems that often the institutional church people from the North brought an order of service, a discipline, and an attitude that removed the laity, especially women, from a freer, more voluntary participation in church affairs and worship that they had known during the days of slavery.

Between the years 1875 and 1885, the black church also began an aggressive, systematic effort to conduct world missions.[27] A number of significant points should be made concerning this statement. The thrust in world or foreign missions commenced in institutional earnest about a decade after Emancipation. Some very interesting explanations present themselves. First, Northern black Christians clearly saw the evangelization and institutionalization of their Southern siblings as paramount. These people represented a huge available field of harvest in reasonable proximity to them. More importantly, they were fellow Afro-Americans; indeed, many in the free churches were actually escaped slaves. Second, Southern blacks who would play a crucial, if not the pivotal role in black foreign mission programs, needed a decade or so to get their feet planted firmly on the ground, so to speak, having recently emerged from slavery. Third, after 1875 the Reconstruction era, which had offered great political and economic promise and racial equality to blacks, was drawing to a close. Given the withdrawal of federal troops from the South and the concomitant rise in white terrorism and economic and political conscription of black Americans, many people of color began to emigrate to other areas of the nation such as Oklahoma and in some cases to other countries. It seems that the thrust in foreign mission represented not only a spiritual yearning to redeem the lost, but a psychological desire to make contacts with peoples and lands with which Afro-Americans could claim an identity.

The predominant, overwhelming concern in world missions were lands with predominantly black populations—the Caribbean and especially Africa. Of course, one would be correct in observing that white mission support and opportunities for black mission endeavors would be greater for black efforts directed to these lands. But as one reads the denominational minutes, newspaper accounts, biographies, autobiographies, and so forth of this period, it becomes very clear that the black church sincerely and passionately desired of its own volition to so direct its programs. We must remember that the concern for African missions—especially—had always been an intense interest for all the black churches. With the abolition of slavery, black Christians now had greater freedom and resources to make concrete their earlier goals. These Christians still believed that God had planned a special destiny for the African race and that they were to be the prime instruments used by him to carry out the divine purpose. If any were prone to forget that heritage, then the contemporary situations of lynching, disenfranchisement, terrorism, economic exploitation, segregation, and so forth which ensued with increasing magnitude after 1875 served to remind them that they were a separate, distinct people. They could not fit comfortably into the American mainstream and develop amnesia concerning their race.

Apparently, the Baptists pioneered in the work of African evangelism.[28] In 1873 the Baptist General Association of Western States and Territories organized in the Midwest and succeeded in placing a few missionaries in Central Africa by the 1880s. In 1879 C. H. Richardson journeyed to the motherland supported in part by the Consolidated American Baptist Convention. It is with William W. Colley, however, that we see perhaps the most influential development in African missions. In 1875 Colley travelled to West Africa jointly supported by his colleagues in the black Virginia Baptist State Convention and the white Southern Baptist Convention. Working under the authority of the white missionary W. J. David of Mississippi, he soon saw the need to organize a separate, national black Baptist convention for foreign missions. Thus, Colley spearheaded the formation of the Baptist Foreign Mission Convention in 1880. This group first commissioned a number of missionaries in 1883. In 1895 the Baptist Foreign Mission Convention united with two other groups to become the National Baptist Convention and continued to operate as the foreign mission board of the new group.

In 1902 Lewis G. Jordan, now the leader of the National Baptist Convention foreign missions program, spoke of the special responsibility that Afro-American Christians had to Africa.

> If the Negro of America will but feel his responsibility and undertake the evangelization of Africa in God's name, unborn millions of Africa's sons will witness a transformed continent. . . . From the great black continents can be carved states or empires, from her cradle will come sons and daughters to rule and reign in the name of Christianity. Negroes of America, God calls you to duty; He calls you to service and He calls you now.[29]

The AMEZ church also joined the postwar quest for the evangelization of Africa.[30] Its pioneering activities centered around Andrew Cartwright. After serving as an organizer of churches in North Carolina, he journeyed to Liberia in January 1876. There he organized churches in Brewerville and Clay Ashland. At the General Conference of 1880, the same year that the BFMC was founded, the Zionites placed their official stamp of endorsement upon the African mission and organized the Woman's Home and Foreign Missionary Society, which raised funds for the cause. Though Cartwright desired the more influential title of presiding elder, he was named superintendent instead and served until 1896. The General

Conference of that year elected John Bryan Small as a bishop and assigned him supervision of churches in portions of Alabama and Mississippi, the West Indies, and Africa. This new bishop took keen interest in the new African mission. Besides calling for increased financial aid to and educated ministers for the stations there, he also visited Africa at least twice before his death in January 1905.

In eulogizing Small, his fellow bishops revealed that the Zionites also shared in the belief that black Christians had a special obligation for African evangelism.

> The claims of Africa upon all Christians, and particularly upon those whose ancestors come from the densely populated continent, are too great and urgent to put aside or turn over to others. Zion has hoisted her banner over the great continent whose sons made one of the largest contributions to the world's earliest civilization and she must see to it that the banner is neither hauled down nor lowered.[31]

The AME church entered the field[32] of African missions somewhat later than the Baptists and the AMEZ. The AMEZ church did not sponsor its first missionary, the Rev. John Richard Frederickson, until January 1886. Fortunately, others in time followed Frederickson, because he in 1899 left the AMEZ and affiliated with the Wesleyan Methodist church. This reluctance or slowness in embarking upon African evangelism reflects the hesitation in certain quarters of the Baptists and the AMEZ as well as the AME churches. Some black Christians undoubtedly saw the need to devote human and financial resources to the vast field here in the states. All the black churches had a long way to go regarding evangelizing, educating, and providing medical service to the millions of Afro-Americans. Why overextend the capacities of the churches, these critics logically reasoned, and inaugurate enterprises thousands of miles overseas?

The 1889 debate between the two AME bishops, Willis Nazery and Daniel Alexander Payne,[33] symbolized the conflict between the pro- and anti-foreign mission elements in various black churches. Both men had been quite active in organizing churches in the states and were clearly dedicated to the cause of evangelism and Christian education. Their difference over African missions revolved around the question of practicality, not theology. Nazery appealed to the time-honored Christian tradition of the Great Commission, arguing that the church had a divine imperative to evangelize lands wherever people were not Christianized. Responsibility did not terminate at one's national boundaries.

Payne expressed great respect for Nazery's zeal, but he claimed that his fellow bishop did not fully appreciate "the cost and difficulties" attendant to the foreign enterprise. Payne responded to his colleague's insistence that the church had an obligation or duty to embark upon world missions.

> Now, where there is no ability to perform an act, there can be no duty to perform it; hence, to exercise a right under such circumstances would place us in a very painful and ridiculous position—even in the position of the man [in a biblical parable attributed to Jesus] who commenced to build, but was not able to finish, his house, and, therefore became the laughingstock of his neighbors.[34]

Payne's argument was very logical. But the expansion of God's church is not primarily contingent upon human logic. He perhaps briefly delayed the AME African mission program, but the call of Africa was too great, with too many of the AME's "neighbors" not laughing at those who would try, but actually answering the call themselves. Once again women arose to champion the cause of evangelism. The Woman's Home and Foreign Missionary Society organized in 1896. This group was established by the General Conference as a direct result of Bishop Henry MacNeal Turner's 1892 trip to Africa.[35] Turner had served in the Reconstruction government in Georgia. His personal experiences of discrimination and those of his fellow blacks in the post-Reconstruction South convinced him that the U.S. would never respect the personhood of blacks. Turning his attention to Africa, he forcefully began to advocate Christianization of, and limited Afro-American emigration to, the mother continent. Reminiscent of pre-Civil War African colonizationists and consistent with the general African mission ideology that had been advocated throughout the century, Turner called for the creation of a "black Christian nation" on the continent. By the time of his death in 1893, even Payne had come to embrace the idea of establishing a school in West Africa for indigenous Africans.[36] This new position was perhaps occasioned by his own personal reflections and meditation upon the matter, the active work of other denominations (including black groups), and the forceful advocacy of Turner.

In Conclusion

We have now come to the end of our foundational story of the black church and evangelism. There are a few points that need to be added. First, we have carried the story of evangelism, home and foreign, to the early 1900s. As the churches continued their activities, the methods further developed and the resources and personnel increased. In other words, as the decades passed, the operations of evangelism became more institutionalized in the churches along with the continuance of the informal methods of personal and communal sharing. Second, a significant introduction to the program of evangelism in the 1920s and 1930s was the advent of gospel music. Many of the more established churches did not receive these new songs of praise (with the rhythmic movement of the singers and the jazz/blues-like sound) with open arms. But Thomas A. Dorsey, the premier gospel writer, Mahalia Jackson,[37] the queen of gospel, and many others understood their task not as one of entertainment but of calling people to embrace the good news. Most certainly, their "performances" and engagements were often revivals by intent and effect.

Our story has provided a brief examination of the evangelism of the black church. In so doing at least three points have emerged. First, there is a rich tradition of black Christian involvement in both domestic and world evangelism. This fact emerges even though we did not discuss in detail the activities of the Christian Methodist

Episcopal church, the Church of God in Christ, and the efforts of black Christians who held membership in predominantly white denominations such as the Episcopalians, Presbyterians, Congregationalists, United Church of Christ, and the Roman Catholics. If we are to discover answers to our problems in the contemporary church, we would be well advised to become cognizant of this legacy of evangelism.

Second, we discovered in the preceding pages that evangelism in the black church (as in other churches) has taken various forms. In some churches evangelism has been formal and institutionalized, such as the organization of home and foreign mission societies; in others evangelism has taken shape in informal ways, such as the spontaneous prayer and praise meetings in slave quarters that resulted in men, women, and children receiving Jesus as Lord and Savior. In the latter instance, we speak of a "family" theology or evangelism where the love of God experienced in the community reaches out and draws the repentant sinner into the community of faith.

Third, we must bear in mind that black Christians were not acting as mere imitators of white churches. Their zeal for mission work was real, not contrived or imitative. Afro-Americans engaged in evangelism for two reasons (there are perhaps others). First, having their hearts touched by the grace of the Savior, they had a sincere desire to fulfill the Great Commission to preach the news of salvation to every creature whether at home or abroad. We must recognize the fact that black Christians truly embraced the faith, not because whites tricked them but because they heard the authentic calling of the real Master. Second, black Christians for much of their history pursued evangelism because they saw a vital connection between embracing the Christian faith and realizing racial progress. They did not transform Jesus' message into a political theology or ideology. However, they firmly believed that Christianity helped people to overcome their spiritual and physical degradation. All descendants of Africa had a common destiny, they said; and they, like some whites, interpreted Psalm 68:31 as a prophecy of the spiritual and political liberation and empowerment of all African peoples. Such a prophecy would be fulfilled through the evangelistic endeavors of Afro-Americans.

CHAPTER 4

Oral Tradition
and Black Evangelistic
Lifestyle

A healthy tradition is vital for the survival of a community. The pioneers of the black church movement in
America passed on to their heirs a rich legacy. The story
in the two preceding chapters clearly shows that black
Christians very early developed a self-understanding in
which they saw themselves as chosen people, believing
that they were far better models of the gospel of Jesus
Christ than their white counterparts. They believed that
God had, through the Union Army's victory in the Civil
War, delivered Afro-American slaves from the clutches of
an avaricious and brutal Pharaoh, just as was done for the
ancient Hebrews.

Engaged in evangelism on the domestic and world
scene, these black Christians established home and foreign mission societies, schools and churches, as agencies
for their organized activity in ministry. Informally, they
spread the good news of God's activity in their lives, in
their families, and communities.

In this chapter I will discuss the concept of oral tradition
with emphasis on its significance in the lives of Afro-
Americans; attention will be given to the transmission and
transition factors in culture; and also a look will be taken
at the components of the black religious experience as
clues to the evangelistic lifestyle.

Oral Tradition

I have already noted previously that every culture or community has some way of transmitting its collective character to succeeding generations. Historically, that has been the role of oral tradition. Oral tradition is the passing on of commonly held values by word of mouth and memory. Long before writing was introduced or the printing press invented, story was the primary vehicle used to transmit legacies. The storyteller may have been officially assigned that role or may have been one of the elders of the tribe, clan, or family. It may have been a nurturing parent. Whatever the agent or status of the storyteller in the community, the transmission was always assured. In ancient Palestine, the storyteller may have been an elder, judge, prophet, priest, rabbi, or scribe. Many African societies had "griots," official storytellers who were the bearers of the tradition. Vested in these persons was the responsibility to tell the legends, old stories, deeds of heroes, and riddles and tales of the tribe, clan, or culture on numerous occasions.

In the telling of the stories, the elders or storytellers were not simply interested in reciting a long series of unrelated events. More importantly, woven into these recollections was an understanding of life and the world based on commonly held perceptions of reality. Themes from past events were recalled to give meaning to some present situation that in turn cast new light on an earlier experience. Thus the story had an ordering of events that gave meaning to the hearer and the tellers. The accounts of ancient Israel, in the telling and retelling of the narratives of the Exodus, took on new meaning as promises for Israel of what was to come upon the return from captivity in Babylon. The early Christian church followed essentially the same pattern. Reading the Old Testament in view of the historical coming of Christ and seeking to understand this event in view of the entire history of a prophetic people, themes were examined in light of the fresh circumstances and then reapplied.

Tradition, which in its original sense meant "to pass on," is more than simply a deposit or repository of accumulated beliefs, values, and ways of doing things. It is an ongoing process of transmission between generations. Often there is the "notion push" that tradition blocks progress or change. While this view is popularly held in some quarters, it represents an inadequate understanding of the special relationship between the two concepts. No such tension really exists. Progress or change is a built-in or necessary characteristic of tradition. To speak of progress as a complete or total change without its historical antecedents runs the serious risk of creating chaos. Without tradition, a people, community, or culture lacks identity and continuity. A people without tradition must live solely in the present with no stream of thought, belief, language, or institution. There is present in their thinking no intellectual or moral scale through which they can evaluate behavior and filter new ideas and understandings. Rites of passage essential for development do not exist. I have already noted that to ignore tradition is a hazardous business. Tradition and progress really are part of the same continuum. As such, tradition has a dynamic quality about it. Frequently the term "living tradition" is used to indicate this quality. A community is shaped and informed by its tradition while at the same time the community shapes and informs that tradition.

Oral tradition then is really the passing on through story of the community's collective character. Alex Haley makes the following comment about the storyteller.

> Then they told me something of which I had never dreamed: of very old men, called griots . . . who were in effect, working archives of oral history . . . who told on special occasions the centuries-old histories of villages, of clans, of families, of great heroes. Throughout the whole of Africa such oral chronicles have been handed down since the time of the ancient forefathers. . . .

> Seeing how astounded I was, these Gambian men reminded me that every living person ancestrally goes back to where no writing existed. The human memory and mouth and ears were the only way these human beings could store and relate information. They said that we who

live in the Western Culture were so conditioned to the crutch of 'a print' that few among us comprehended what a trained memory was capable of.[1]

The memory as well as the mouth has a crucial role in preserving and passing on stories. The talmudic tradition that existed in Israel grew out of a practice of training disciples to pass on tradition by memory. "Talmud" means "learned by heart."[2] Even in the early church, worshipers preferred to hear the sayings of Jesus as recalled by the Apostle.[3]

With the African griots as well as some biblical tradition, memory is a powerful instrument for maintaining and passing on stories of the culture. Indeed, as Soggins notes, it was only through oral tradition that the literature of Israel survived the catastrophes of 587 B.C. and 70 A.D.[4] The Western mindset has difficulty understanding the importance of the trained memory. In fact, perhaps the closest associations in our culture that would indicate how important these elements are would be the value we place upon libraries, archives, museums, and now computers. These are places/machines where the repository of Western culture is maintained. In the East, learning by memory still occurs and is a normal way of transmitting long text.

Haley notes for us what is involved in the training of the storyteller:

> A senior griot would be a man usually in his late 60s or early 70s; below him would be progressively younger griots—and apprenticing boys, so a boy would be exposed to those griots' particular line of narratives for 40 or 50 years before he could qualify as a senior griot.[5]

As noted by Haley, when the storyteller had the responsibility for official documents such as births, deaths, marriages, and so forth, conscious stress was placed upon accuracy, content, and form as the extensive griot training indicates. The tradition would best tell the what of events without necessarily indicating the how or why. Other stories, however, while remaining for centuries, developed variations as the storytellers recalled themes to deal with fresh events. It must be kept in mind that a tradition lives as long as there are practical, sociological, religious, or ideological entries connected with it.[6]

Some scholars have argued that the African slaves arrived on the shores of the American continent without a common tradition, common language, or common memory—as blank entities distinguished only by dark complexion and tropical temperament. Lacking a tradition or culture or identity, the African slave was singled out among the divergent new settlers on the American scene. The chief proponent of this theory, Robert Parks, writes

> Other people have lost, under the disintegrating influence of the American environment, much of their cultural heritage. None have been so utterly cut-off and estranged from their ancestral land, tradition and people.[7]

The views of Parks and E. Franklin Frazier, while dominating much of twentieth-century scholarship, also foster the notion that Afro-Americans developed a cultural dependence on their white masters. In responding to Frazier and Parks, James Washington observes

> . . . slave children and adults have to think hard and quickly in order to survive the often intentional yet sometimes unwitting attempt to destroy their African cultural heritage. To argue that this heritage either stayed intact or was totally destroyed, is thoroughly to misconstrue the dialectics of cultural contacts.[8]

Though this view pushed by Parks and Frazier has been discredited in recent scholarship, it still has currency in mass culture. In a discussion with a Native American colleague a few years ago, I was surprised to learn that the Navaho word for "black American" was literally translated to mean "white-black man." Such an understanding is but a microcosm of the view that black Americans, void of any cultural heritage of their own, are imitators of white Americans. The more subtle manifestation of this view is the notion that the only difference between white churches and black churches is that the latter are composed of blacks. Thus in developing resources for churches and training and equipping leadership, the presupposition still holds that the black church movement is at best a protest movement against racism in white churches. Notation here is made not for detailed discussion of the issues involved, rather, it is made to further support the need for black Americans to recover a living tradition.

I have already noted that Parks's theory represents a major bias in current scholarship. Lawrence Levine puts the matter into perspective.

> To insist that only those elements of slave culture were African which remain largely unchanged from the African past is to misinterpret the nature of culture itself. Culture is not a fixed condition, but a process: the product of interaction between past and present. Its toughness and resiliency are determined not by a culture's ability to withstand change, which indeed may be a sign of stagnation, not life, but its ability to react creatively and responsibly to the realities of a new situation. The question . . . is not of survival but of transformation.[9]

If Levine's perspective is correct, then the African slaves shut out of American life, insulated in slavery on the plantation, rejected the understanding placed upon them by a slave culture. These men and women demonstrated great resiliency and imagination as they developed a world view rooted not only in the African but also the American consciousness. This new world view was expressed most creatively in black religious life.

Even to claim that the slaves were imitators is to misunderstand the nature of experience and personhood. It also misconstrues the role of world view in tradition. Each individual has a perception of reality that differs from the rest of the world. The filters through which the individual understands his or her experience allow personal histories to become as unique as fingerprints. While there are similarities in experience, no two histories are identical. Thus, personality represents interest, habits, likes, dislikes, and rules of behavior that are distinctive. Bandler and Grinder relate

> Two identical twins might grow up together in the same home with the same parents, having almost identical experiences, but each in the process of watching their par-

ents relate to each other and the rest of the family might model their experience differently. One might say: My parents never loved each other very much . . . , while the other might say: My parents really cared about each other . . . , thus even in the limiting case of identical twins, their experiences as persons will give rise to differences in the way they create their perceptions of the world.[10]

If this is the case for identical twins, then for unrelated persons the differences will be more pervasive. My point here simply is that black slaves were human beings with personalities of their own. They were not like blank entities upon which some cultural stamp could be placed. Many scholars fail to acknowledge that discussions in the realm of the conscious and unconscious mind are very much the property of subjective reasoning. Mircea Eliade questions whether justifiable distinctions still can be made between the conscious and the subconscious. He has offered another concept called transconsciousness.[11] Henry Mitchell suggests that Eliade's concept of one consciousness can be applied to the collective world view of Afro-Americans. He further describes it as a multichannel awareness and integration that manifests itself in a mystical unity experienced in worship.[12]

One must keep in mind that African slaves had been in the United States one hundred years before significant numbers were converted to Christianity. While most commentators write of the lack of a common language among the slaves, the fact that neither white evangelists nor slaveholders spoke any of the languages of the slaves cannot be overlooked. The Bishop of London, writing in a letter of 1727 noted, "They (the African slaves) are utter strangers to our language and we to theirs; and the gift of tongues being now ceased, there is no means left of instructing them in the doctrines of the Christian religion."[13] Indeed, the reports from missionaries working with the slaves cited little success with the African-born slaves. The Bishop would write further

Many of the Negroes who [were] grown persons when they came over, do of themselves obtain so much of our language as to enable them to understand and to be understood in things which concern the ordinary business of life.[14]

Years ago when I was in undergraduate school, a history professor invited a well-known scholar to address his class in Negro history during Negro History Week (as it was then called). During his lecture, the scholar commented that his research in oral history had led him to the conclusion that the house slaves were more likely to be leaders than those who worked in the fields. That observation, among others, prompted a lively discussion at the close of the lecture. When questioned about some of his conclusions, the scholar became quite agitated. Finally, one of the students, sensing that he was on to something, pressed the visiting historian about his methods of research. Much to our amazement, it was discovered after considerable discussion that there was no factual basis for the conclusion that leadership was more prevalent among house slaves than those who worked in the fields. Often in Western scholarship the assumption is made that the absence of knowledge means *absence thereof.*

The fact that that many eyewitnesses wrote commentaries on the life and thought of African slaves without knowledge of their languages is indicative of the extent of the limitations of such scholarship.

Aldous Huxley makes this perception on this point.

> Each person is at each moment capable of remembering all that has ever happened to him and of perceiving everything that is happening everywhere else in the universe. The function of the brain and the nervous system is to protect us from being overwhelmed and confused by this mass . . . of knowledge, by shutting out most of what we should otherwise perceive and remember at any moment and leaving only a very small special selection. . . . Accordingly each of us is potentially Mind-at-Large . . . to make biological survival possible Mind-at-Large has to be funneled through the reducing valve of the brain and nervous system. What comes out at the other end is . . . a trickle of the kind of consciousness which helps us to stay alive. . . . To formulate and express the contents of this reduced awareness, man has invented and endlessly elaborated upon those symbol systems and implicit philosophies which we call languages. Each individual is . . . the beneficiary . . . of the tradition into which he has been born.[15]

If Huxley is correct, then the transmission of the tradition occurs through stories in the language of the community into which we are born, using the symbols and images of that community. Since tradition possesses a world view, that is a perception of reality that orders life so as to make sense. Henry Mitchell is correct when he notes "that the world view of African-Americans was communicated in the earliest years through the limited contact of parents with their children."[16]

I agree with Levine's conclusion that what is important in this transmittal process is not survival but transformation. To suggest that slavery existed without African culture and to make that idea central in an intellectual debate based on accounts from eyewitnesses who neither spoke the languages of the Africans nor were aware of their customs, but wrote their account through the eyes of outsiders, is an interesting twist in scholarship to say the least. As human beings Africans held the world view that had been transmitted by their own language. As they learned to speak the language of their new land in the succeeding years, even though they were isolated from the larger American scene, their world view was transformed. Shut out of the developing American community, slaves forged their own community. With the basic family utterly destroyed by the systematic effort to "thingify" all human life in their community, the slaves developed a family built around the entire community.

This isolation allowed slaves to maintain a unity of life quite apart from the Western dichotomy of the sacred and the secular. For the African, humankind lived constantly in the presence of the divine; all of time and space is sacred. To the African, life is lived in the religious universe; one participates from birth to death in the religious drama. Sacredness to the African mind-set has little to do with the rejection of the world; rather, it is inclusion of all aspects of this world and life within the religious universe. Worship for the African occurs at any time in any place. There are no rules requiring people to worship at a given time and place. God is omnipresent, reachable at any time

in any place. People worship whenever and wherever the
need arises. John Mbiti concludes

> . . . to African people this is a deeply religious universe
> whether it is viewed in terms of time or space, and human
> life is a religious experience of that universe. So Africans
> find or attribute religious meaning to the whole of exis-
> tence.[17]

Often, attempts to interpret African life result in impos-
ing a Western mindset upon traditions and beliefs that are
alien. In all cases attempts must be made to discover the
meaning of practices and beliefs to the people with whom
they originate rather than what they seem to appear to
mean in Western eyes.

Levine notes that the slaves' understanding of the universe was evidenced in the spirituals. Spirituals were sung
anywhere, any time. He observes "the songs of God and
the mythic heroes of their religion were not confined to
a specific time or place, but were appropriate to almost
every situation."[18] This unity of life becomes central to a
discussion of the lifestyles and methods of evangelism
within the slave community.

For the most authentic rendering of black religious life,
one must look at life in the slave community on the plantation. It was here that the black church movement as an
invisible institution developed what shall be called an
evangelistic lifestyle, that is, a natural way of living and
acting evangelistically.

It has already been noted that most evangelism for the
Afro-American slaves occurred in the context of a caring,
nurturing community that in many ways was similar to
the Christian community in the apostolic and subapostolic
age. These communities were characterized by mutual
sharing and an extended family that included relatives,
friends, and elders. While worship was important to the
life of the community, it occurred in several settings.
There was the Sunday worship, usually required of all
slaves, which included visiting white preachers and occasionally a slave preacher. More popular among the slaves
were their own informal prayer meetings that occurred in
secret places, the "hush harbours," the field, in cabins, in

slave quarters, and sometimes in several cabins in the quarters. Frequently these prayer meetings would last all night. If there was a slave preacher present he would preach, but most often they shared these meetings among themselves.

These meetings were characterized by freedom of expression in the singing, praying, and shouting. Prayers were often especially for "mourners"—those seekers who had not yet had a conversion experience. As a caring, nurturing community, these seekers received support not only through the prayers but also from spiritual guides, who were usually elderly men and women who had the respect of the entire community. There also were "watchmen" who were religious leaders on the plantation. According to Raboteau, their duties included "advising on spiritual matters, opening and leading prayer meetings, counseling 'mourners,' sinners seeking conversion and generally setting Christian examples for the slaves."[19]

The conversion experience of slaves varied sometimes. Sometimes it happened suddenly while they were alone, and at other times sinners became seekers on the mourners' bench at prayer meetings. Many of the conversion stories told indicated a period of anxiety prior to the actual experience. Raboteau discovered parallels in the structure and patterns of the conversion stories told by many slaves. He offers this description: "First a feeling of sinfulness, then a vision of damnation and finally an experience of acceptance by God and being reborn or made new."[20]

Some conversion experiences were accompanied by visions with images from the Bible, especially from Revelations. These images were from sermons or spirituals and from "experience meetings" where other conversion stories had been told.

Baptism followed the conversion experience. The following description was indicative of the sense of change attached to this experience.

When I got to be a big boy, my Ma got religion at the camp meeting at El-bethel. She shouted and sung for three days, going all over the plantation and the neighboring ones, inviting her friends to come and see her baptized and shouting and praying for dem. She went around to all the people that she had done wrong and begged their forgiveness. She sent for dem that had wronged her and told dem dat she was born again and a new woman and dat she would forgive dem. She wanted every body dat was not saved to go up wid her. . . . My Ma took me wid her to see her baptized, and I was so happy that I sung and shouted wid her.[21]

The above quote shows the importance of baptism in the religious life of the slave as well as the informal sharing of the good news on a personal basis. Remarkably like many in the early church, the personal testimony was an integral part of the life of the slave. The experience meetings mentioned earlier were the settings of public personal testimonies as well as the prayer meetings and worship services.

The slave preacher was a trusted member of the religious life of the community. His work and role in boldly speaking of God's liberating activity in present and future history, once out from under the watchful eye of whites, is well documented. Black preachers were trusted also because of their powerful preaching.

De preacher I liked de best was named Mathew Ewing. He was comely . . . Black as night, and he sure could read out of his hand. He never learned no real readin and writin but he sure knowed his Bible and would hold his hand out and make like he was readin, and preach de puriest preachin' you ever heard.[22]

It has already been noted that the slaves preferred their own preachers. The sermons of the black preacher were based upon the Bible. Though many in the slave community could not read, their sermons were filled with biblical stories, characters, and images. Scholars have concluded that the biblical orientation of slave religion was its central characteristic.[23] Raboteau reports that illiteracy did not prevent the slaves from learning about the Bible. The Bible became a part of their oral tradition, and they committed it to memory. Missionaries to the plantation were in awe of the slaves' ability to remember chapter after chapter of Scripture.[24]

Woven into the fabric of life on the plantation were the spirituals. More detailed discussion of the meaning of spirituals will appear in Chapter 5. Here, however, the spiritual is viewed as a manifestation of the communal nature of the black slave community. Created by the community to be an expression in a communal setting, the spirituals encompassed many of the stories of the community while at the same time expressing deep truths about the community's story as it encountered the Christian story.

What we have seen up to this point is that the community used several methods of evangelism, including public and personal evangelism. In the area of public evangelism, there were testimonies, preaching, public worship, prayer meetings, experience meetings, and regular Sunday worship as well as conversion stories. Personal evangelism was primarily done through mutual storytelling and story listening. All of this was done in the context of a caring, nurturing community. The influence of this community was strong to the extent that the seeker sought out the community. In this setting the seeker found a non-threatening, supportive environment or hospitality in which the person could be counseled on matters of interpretation, listened to and comforted as the seeker journeyed through the wilderness or valley experience, watched over in prayer and told the stories of members of the community of faith. It was also a community that validated the pilgrim's personal encounter with God.

It is clear that black churches engaged in numerous activities for the purposes of evangelism. It is accurate, further, to conclude that independent black churches in the North and those independent denominations that developed before and after the Civil War were more likely to be involved in organized activity for the spreading of the gospel. Early in their development these churches formed mission societies and developed connectional relationships or conventions to support mission activity for the spreading of the good news of God's work in their lives. Through that thrust their evangelistic activity took on a unique character with the blending of evangelical Christianity, the black world view, and the struggle for liberation and wholeness in a hostile environment. The structures developed were similar to those of their white counterparts, although black Baptists would later form national organizations well before their white brethren.

It should be clear to the reader now that there is a tradition of evangelism in the black church. The pioneers of this tradition followed through on their mission of preaching the gospel to their brothers and sisters who had not heard. While they were small in number, they did not separate their interior institutional life from its mission in and on behalf of the world. They believed that their mission consisted of the task of freeing black folks' souls from sin and their bodies from physical, political, and social oppression, and of setting conditions of existence so that they could achieve their full humanity. It was a special calling from God that had been thrust upon them. They responded with joy and enthusiasm.

CHAPTER 5

The Meaning of the Story

I should have begun this book with a story. The human spirit has an insatiable fascination with story. A good story always captures and holds the reader's or listener's attention.

On several occasions during workshops on evangelism, I have asked participants to recall who or what was significant in bringing them to the Christian faith—a simple assignment. It required no writing, just a good memory. The stories that emerged seemed endless. Everyone loves a good story. We remember them more than sermons, lectures, or doctrines of the faith.

In this chapter I shall discuss the nature and function of story, spirituals as a communal expression of the story, and recovery of your own story for evangelism. In Chapter 1 story was described as an imaginative way of ordering our experience in such a way as to give past events power and meaning to the hearer. Our imagination is at work in story. It is the property of the community and uses the language, images, and symbols of that community. It allows a community to tell themselves, their children, and the world their perception of reality. The black American community, as all communities, is a story-shaped community. A community cannot avoid telling its own story. Self-understanding, beliefs, and attitudes are passed on through the telling of stories. Stories come in many forms: songs, tales, legends, jokes, and even gossip. Story is how we live.

The Nature of Story

At least two critical issues arise here that must be addressed. First, if story is the product of the imagination, how do we distinguish it from the imaginary or fantasy? Second, how can one know that his or her personal story interconnects with the Christian story?

Crucial to any discussion of story is some distinction between imagination and the imaginary. Essentially, as I already have noted, imagination represents the constructive, creative powers of the mind. Within the mind mental images occur that influence our attitudes, health, and spiritual and daily lives. The mental images follow our sense perceptions of taste, smell, sight, hearing, and feeling. The imagination brings an image to the mind so that it can be pondered or examined. Recently a friend was asked to recall some images of his first child. He paused for a moment and then started to smile. He heard the sound of his son crying and laughing. If someone asks the number of rooms in your home, you would probably form a picture and then count the rooms in your house in your mind. The mind has this ability to form mental images. One of the ministers of my childhood often used the expression "in my mind's eye." Interestingly, that is what the imagination is: a way of seeing. Thus, in the imagination we move beyond what society or culture tells us in the socialization process in order to find a perspective for ourselves. Indeed, the mind is able to see, not just to look. When Jesus encountered the rich young ruler who asked how he might inherit eternal life, the Master's answer caused the young man to leave with a heavy heart; "for he was a man of great wealth" (Matthew 19:22, *The Jerusalem Bible*). He lacked imagination.

The imaginary, on the other hand, is fantasy—the unreal. Fantasy, too, is composed of mental images. But they are not a part of a world of facts, truth, or reality. William F. Fore makes the following point.

Sherwood Schwartz writes and produces . . . "Gilligan's Island," a comedy originated in the 1960s in which a zany group of castaways manages to survive not only a shipwreck, but each other. Schwartz tells of having received in 1964 a visit from a Commander Dole of the U.S. Coast Guard (who) presented Schwartz with a batch of telegrams.

While the wording of the telegrams varied, they in substance said the same thing: "for several weeks now, we have seen American citizens stranded on some Pacific Island. We spend millions in foreign aid. Why not send one U.S. Destroyer to rescue those poor people before they starve to death?"[1]

Gilligan's Island was part of the make-believe world of television. Yet dozens of concerned citizens were unable to make that distinction. That is fantasy. Fantasy moves into a destructive, confused world where facts, truth, and reality have no jurisdiction. Imagination, however, is constructive and creative. It builds on knowledge and does not break completely with one's environment. Story, in a word, results from imagination, not fantasy.

In the second matter, the critical issue is how I can be sure my story meets and joins the Christian story, or, how to use the issue of truthfulness in story so as to avoid self-deception. Sallie Te Selle shares:

We all love a good story because of the basic narrative quality of human experience; in a sense, any story is a story about ourselves, and a good story is good precisely because somehow it rings true to human life. Human life is not marked by instantaneous rapture and easy solutions. Life is tough. . . . We recognize our pilgrimages from here to there in a good story; we feel its movement in our bones and know it is "right." We love stories then, because our lives are stories and in an attempt to move, temporarily and painfully, we recognize our own story. For the Christian, the story of Jesus is the story par excellence. That God should be with us in the story of a human life could seem as a happy accident, but it makes more sense to see it as God's way of always being with human beings as they are—as concrete, temporal beings who have a beginning and an end—who are . . . stories themselves.[2]

Succinctly, the story of God's loving activity for thousands of years and the ultimate expression of it in Jesus Christ is a good story—a story par excellence. It is a historical and universal story. It grabs us instinctively. We see it as our story, too! It is the incarnate God coming to us human beings in flesh and blood and sinew, taking our fragmented, broken stories and giving them new meaning, power, and vitality. Story, then, is a part of revelation. In other words, I am a product of my community. My story is composed of my personal vision, drawn from my most intimate communities and beyond. Therefore, my story constitutes the filters of being an American black male and a rural Southerner who is also a baby boomer. The interpersonal, nonverbal subjectivity of the self is drawn into the creative, transforming encounter with Ultimate Reality; the self dies to its own will and is resurrected selfless to the all-encompassing will of Ultimate Reality. In this intensely intimate experience, the self has participated in the revelatory experience. My experience of God's disclosure is told in the language of my community, using the images and world views of that community for articulation.

Such was the nature of the spiritual in the life of the Afro-American slave community. In the spiritual the slave story of God's self-disclosure was told in the language of the community using the images and world views of that community. Spirituals were communal songs that engaged its singers in a ritual. Whether in the fields, praise meetings, or worship services, the lyrics were acted out or dramatized by the bands of shouters. Many of the slaves claimed that older slaves would make up the spirituals on the spur of the moment. What is clear is that spirituals had a flexible, improvisational pattern that allowed an individual slave or a specific event/experience to become a part of the song. Of course, this was communal. As the shouter would interject some experience of joy or sorrow, the experience would be shared by the community. Thus, the community could associate and finally identify with the joy and sorrow of the shouter. In reenacting the theme of the spiritual, the shouter would stand outside his or her self. The experience symbolically became the community's, thus validating the individual believer's involvement in the caring-supportive community.

As any good story the spiritual was like a vessel that enclosed a deeper meaning. Raboteau suggests "spirituals followed a pattern found in much of the verbal art of West Africa and many folk tales of their American descendants where indirect, veiled social comment and criticism are prevalent."[3]

With this in mind, it is conceivable that some might possibly misconstrue the meaning of the spiritual, especially as code songs. This much should be added: With their flexibility and constant changing of lyrics, the meaning of the spiritual would surely change as well.

However, steeped in African and biblical traditions, the spiritual constantly renewed the revelatory experiences of the community. In worship experience the contact between God and humankind became a living reality to the slave. Because the slave had an African concept of time and identified so closely with the children of Israel, events and characters from the Bible were alive and present and part of their community. (The African concept of time is quite different from Western concepts of time. African time is two-dimensional, with a long past, a present, and virtually no future. At best, in the African mind-set the future might be called "potential time." Actual time begins with the present and moves backward into the past. John Mbiti uses the words *Sasa* and *Zamani* to identify Little-Time [*Sasa*] and Big-Time [*Zamani*]. Events move backwards, therefore, Little-Time is a part of Big-Time and feeds it and eventually disappears into it. For a more detailed discussion, read Mbiti's *African Religions and Philosophy*.) Since time and events moved backwards, the slave community was not encumbered by these barriers. Thus, the heroes of the Bible were to them a part of their community. Jacob, Moses, Joshua, and Daniel were heroes who had withstood the test of time. "Weeping Mary" and "Doubting Thomas" were community members who had withstood trials. The themes of these narratives were indicative of the tests and trials the slaves themselves faced. As they recalled these themes, it gave them new hope for their situation and the stories gave new power and meaning. Jesus, the Suffering Servant, was an ever-present and intimate friend.

> He had been wid us, Jesus.
> He still be wid us, Jesus.
> He will be wid us, Jesus.
> Be wid us to the end.[4]

The spiritual taught the sinner caught outside "the ark of safety" to turn, be convicted of sin, and repent. The invitations were many, "Sinner, Please Don't Let This Harvest Pass," "Turn Sinner, Turn Today," "Come and Go to That Land Where I'm Bound," "Let Jesus Lead You," "You Must Have That Pure Religion," all show the impossibility of escape for the sinner.

> You must have that pure religion.
> You must have religion and your soul converted.
> You must have that pure religion, can't cross here.
> Oh, where you running sinner you can't cross here.
> You may run to the river of Jordan, you can't cross here.
> Oh, sinner, you must have that pure religion.
> You must have religion and your soul converted.
> You must have that pure religion. You can't cross here.[5]

Spirituals would combine the images of divine mercy and apocalyptic judgment to convince the sinner to seek conversion. For the difficult and lonely wilderness experience that each mourner would have to go through, the spirituals would implore him or her to "Go Down in De Lonesome Valley," or out into the wilderness "To Wait Upon the Lord" for "He will take away the sins of the world." The pilgrimage to "The Lonesome Valley" was necessary for the guilt-laden mourner or seeker to go through. The individual mourner was expected to literally wander through the woods seeking "to get right with God." During revivals and prayer meetings, elder Christians would gather around the mourners to sing and pray all night. This practice still was very much evident in black religious life in rural Mississippi during my childhood; however, the services did not last all night. After conversion and entry into the community of faith through baptism, the spirituals nurtured, exhorted, and prepared the slaves for death where they would be free in heaven. The River Jordan, symbolic of death, represented the last great barrier to freedom.

> Deep river, my home is over Jordan;
> Deep river, my home is over Jordan.
> Oh, don't you want to go to that gospel feast,
> That promised land where all is peace?
> Deep river, I want to cross over into the campground.[6]

From birth to freedom the spirituals used biblical themes that told of a God whose activity in the community was immediate and intense. To many slaves who were unable to read and write, the spirituals had the currency of theology. The spirituals were, in a word, good stories that helped the slaves recognize their pilgrimage from here to there. They also helped them to know that God comes to us in a human life and also stays with us.

The Function of Story

Story is the only vehicle in which the very meaning of life is embodied. In order for us to know ourselves amidst the incompleteness, paradoxes, uncertainty, and ambiguity in which we live, we need story.

Let me try to illustrate my point by referring again to the spirituals. In the environment in which the slaves found themselves, all the apparent forces of life conspired to rob them of their belief that they were persons of worth and dignity. Every pulse of the society, every act of the systematic enslavement, tried to engrain into their minds that they were "things"—properties. Even propagandists operating under the guise of missionaries preached that God wanted this enslavement, that it was divinely ordained. Over against this terrible background was the word coming from the community of faith: "you are not slaves; you are God's children." In the creative, constructive powers of their minds, the slaves took images from the Old and New Testament, the world of nature, and the personal religious experiences of members of their community and told the stories of their communities.

> When Israel was in Egypt's land;
> Let my people go,
> Oppressed so hard they could not stand,
> Let my people go.
> Go down, Moses, 'way down in Egypt's land.
> Tell old Pharaoh, Let my people go!
> Thus said the Lord, bold Moses said;
> Let my people go,
> If not, I'll smite your firstborn dead,
> Let my people go.
> No more shall they in bondage toil,
> Let my people go,
> Let them come out with Egypt's spoil,
> Let my people go.
> The Lord told Moses what to do;
> Let my people go,
> To leave the children of Israel thro'
> Let my people go.
> When they had reached the other shore;
> Let my people go,
> They sang a song of triumph o'er,
> Let my people go.[7]

The story told of oppression, frustration, and divine deliverance. Though the slave was not delivered, these spirituals spoke to deep needs in life.

> My Lord delivered Daniel,
> My Lord delivered Daniel,
> My Lord delivered Daniel,
> Why can't He deliver me?[8]

The spiritual "Go Down, Moses" recounts the story of the enslavement of the children of Israel. Moses was sent by God and instructed on what to do. After procrastinating tactics by the oppressor, he led the Israelites to freedom where songs of triumph were sung. It is a story in which God acted in a time of trial and oppression. The slaves who sang about it believed and trusted that God would act again in new circumstances. The theme of Daniel is similar, for there is triumph and deliverance. Howard Thurman persuasively makes the point that for the slave

God was the deliverer . . . it was a faith that makes much in contemporary life that goes under that name seem like filthy rags. Daring to believe that God cared for them despite the cruel vicissitudes of life meant the giving of wings to life that nothing could destroy. This is the basic affirmation of all high religion.[9]

Earlier in the quote from Sallie Te Selle the phrase "we recognize our pilgrimage from here to there in a good story" was noted. Life is a pilgrimage from here to there, a journey from the memory of the known into the unknown. The historical-universal story mediates between humankind and the unknown and the person who tells the story becomes the human mediator.

Howard Thurman suggests that the pilgrim says "yes" at pivotal points in life without always knowing why and at some point arrives at a place where he or she recognizes "that I have been coming here all my life and did not know it."[10] That is, in fact, the pilgrimage "into the lonesome valley or through the wilderness" that every Christian must take. In the journey we face the temptations of the wilderness, die to our own self-will, and in selflessness experience new birth in community as radically free sons and daughters of God. There is a power in this radical new freedom. John Dunne describes it precisely.

> . . . the power of the whole man. The power that is more powerful than either flesh or spirit—that power, the power of the new man within him appears to be in fact the power of God at work within Him, for it does what the power of the Creator would do.[11]

The pilgrimage from here to there is more than the movement from birth to death. It includes, in the words of Urban T. Holmes III, "the ability to live for another, to live for value and to live for the end."[12]

For the slave the journey from here to there was a pilgrimage that led inevitably to God, as the spirituals clearly expressed. Every story has to have an ending. The slaves did not find resolution in the story—resolution was found in God. Thus, as radically free sons and daughters of God, the persistent self-image that the slaves shared in the spirituals was that of a chosen people.

Story is essential for life; without story we live in an unreal world. Living as we do in a highly literate, technologically advanced society, the tendency is to believe that story is childlike. While Jesus made having a childlike spirit a condition for entry into the kingdom, my point here is that there is a prevalent belief that an intellectually better account can be given than that which stories provide. Thus, we try to make the point without story; we seek to explain. Story, however, is not explanation. Story is meaning. There are two areas of speaking in which explanation is grossly inadequate: speech about the human self and speech about God.

Try for a moment to explain who you are. Almost instantaneously you become involved in a description of qualities and attributes about yourself. There is something about your particular uniqueness that defies explanation. It is only when you start to share your autobiography that people will come to know who in fact you are. What is true of the human self is also true, I believe, when we attempt to speak of God. When we speak of God we speak usually of concepts and universals, as though God were somehow an indefinite noun. God, however, is a proper name, a name not held by anyone else or anything else. A proper name is unique and that uniqueness cannot be universalized. My contention is that as with the human self, so also with God. To speak of God is to speak in stories. Finally, to speak of God is to speak of relationship, otherwise one finds oneself dealing with abstractions.

The coming of God in a human life is the content of the Christian story. It is also a story of relationship. When the story comes to us the response is one of transrationality rather than rationality. That is, our rational responses are commonsense, thinking responses. There is a concern for certainty, familiarity, or familiar ground and security. The transrational response, on the other hand, is a feeling, intuitive response. It entails ambiguity, risks, and the unknown. The city is the symbol of the rational. The wilderness is symbolic of the transrational. Our pilgrimage through life moves in and out of these two polarities. In the feeling, intuitive response, one looks for meaning. The common sense thinking response is explanation. Put these two distinctions into the language of story and you have the closed story (rational) and the open story (transrational).

A closed story may have begun as an open story, but the original revelatory experience has been codified. It is the creed, the formula in which no word or image can be changed. It is once and for all times engraved in stone. In human life the closed story has no tension with the gospel story. It is not the story that gets us from here to there. The closed story is generally a product of a highly literate, rational society.

On the other hand, the open story remains imaginative, always developing, capable of making the pilgrimage with us, providing exhortation and nurture. The open story is never finished. The spirituals and the gospels are open stories. They are parables. They live with uncertainty and ambiguity, with paradox and the absurd. Their resolution is in God.

Discovering the Story

Earlier I spoke of God's advent in a human life as a good story. As a good story, it captures our attention and fascinates our imagination. The Advent is a good story also because it shows us what God has done in the past in Jesus Christ. God will act again even in different situations. That is the message of the *kerygma*. It is the good news of the gospel. It was the meaning of the spirituals. It is the Christian story, the story of the black church. It is also my story.

The story of Jesus, like a story par excellence, grabs us at the level of feeling. We feel its movement in our bones and know it is right. We love it because our lives are stories, too, and his story becomes our story. It is not through propositional formulas or doctrinal truths that we respond to the story.

When the spirituals were sung, they showed the interrelatedness of the story of Jesus with Afro-American culture. Thus the hearer could connect his or her vision and be called to repentance and faith. In this we see three stories—Jesus' story, the culture story, and the hearer's story (or my story)—all of which are open to the vision of God. We have to attempt to unite these visions by interrelating stories.

There is little difficulty in identifying the story of Jesus. For black Americans there is the critical question of how to identify our cultural and personal stories. This is a difficult problem. It is also a problem of interpretation. We do not lack for stories to tell. The first reason we find it difficult to identify our stories is that we have not been fed a diet of consistent stories. Stories are basically oral in nature and lead to the written story; but storytellers, even story readers who read aloud are not as common as one might hope in black American families. Coupled with this there is the constant diet of television that has become the chief storyteller and mythmaker in our time. More on this will be discussed in Chapter 6. For many black Americans, living and surviving in the hostile environment of America has been a painful experience. Some persons have sought to bury that pain without realizing that in closing it off they also close off a portion of their pilgrimage. The gentleman to whom I referred in Chapter 1 becomes an example of this situation. A traumatic experience happened in his life more than fifty years ago. It was so traumatic that, in order to survive, he sealed off the pain so that not even his wife was aware of that emotional experience. When he recalled it the experience was fresh in his memory. Not all experiences, however, are or have been traumatic. On countless occasions I have watched persons get in touch with their stories and watched the emotions expressed clearly in their faces. This leads me to the second problem we have with good stories: they expose us. As characteristic of a dying to self-control, they require that we reveal our most intimate childlike qualities and trust. Our whole culture and especially the hostile environment that black

Americans find themselves in condition us against this. However, if we do not tell stories, our imaginations become rusty from disuse. The critical task for ministry in the black church is to teach black Americans to get their stories together.

CHAPTER 6

Renewing the Story

*I*n a discussion not long ago regarding the contents of this book, a friend, the pastor of a large urban congregation in an eastern city, asked me a pointed question. "What has the tradition of spirituals and conversion stories from the eighteenth and nineteenth centuries to do with urban black poor people and young upwardly mobile black professionals?" It was a fair question, although I really had not anticipated it. I found myself brooding for days, and then it came to me. It has everything to do with it. I realized that I heard the question put a little differently some years before at a convocation on evangelism at Howard University, when a pastor asked, "How does one minister to this 'new Negro?'" Then I realized it is the critical task facing the tradition in its new context. It is a task I shall attempt to address in this chapter.

The vibrant, militant institution that was spawned out of the union of independent black churches of the North and those of their Southern kindred marched into the Reconstruction and post-Reconstruction eras as mighty forces for the Lord. With a clarity of mission and identity, these churches evangelized multitudes, started new churches, commissioned missionaries, established schools and hospitals, formed burial societies and insurance companies, and watched over their newly freed flocks. They were active in civil rights and politics. Indeed, they were evangelizing, caring fellowships that did not make a distinction between their interior institutional life and their mission for their black brothers and sisters. They were responding to God's call with a purposefulness and fervor.

However, it was not to last. Expanding rapidly, these militant churches were soon to face struggles that would drain their strength and energies. Faced with betrayal and outright collusion on the part of government and political officials, the rise of organized terrorist activity represented in the main by the Ku Klux Klan, and the legalization of segregation, these new churches would stretch to their seams. At the same time, the accommodationist philosophy of Booker T. Washington and the Tuskegee machine would move in to fill the void left by militant leadership. The violence against black Americans would grow unchecked by any legal authority. The Rev. Emmanuel Love would express the frustration generally held by black leaders in a letter to a national church newspaper.

> We look to God and ask what are we to do? What is the use of appealing to the government? Our sufferings and inhuman outrages are known. The crimes are not committed in a corner. The men were not masked. The government [has] known our condition. The government protects its citizens abroad. It does seem that the glory of American citizenship means no glory for us. What are we to do?[1]

The newly found freedom of black Americans would soon turn into a "veil of tears." With the onslaught of Jim Crow legislation throughout the South, validated by the separate-but-equal decision of the Supreme Court, newly legalized segregation became an extension of the outlawed system of slavery. Roaming lynch mobs, race riots, and a general atmosphere of unchecked, pervasive violence was the setting in which black churches now found themselves. This extreme hostility, coupled with a massive social upheaval caused by the migration of Southerners to the cities, the Great Depression, and the pathologies of urban ghetto living began to strain what was once a vibrant, enthusiastic movement. Gayraud S. Wilmore wrote

Shorn of roots in the militant black church of the nine-teenth century, black Christians turned inward to find a white Americanized Jesus—the image of their psychic void—and traditional spirituality became uncoupled from a sense of historical cultural vocation of the black church to transform the whole of black life.[2]

Indeed, this identity crisis of black Christians was simply a microcosm of what was happening in the larger black American community. Despite the perpetual identity crisis facing black churches, the drift by some churches into a moralistic, otherworldly revivalism, a creeping secularism invading black communities, a penchant on the part of some churches for a "blackenized" version of fundamentalism, and the sapping of energies in trivial internecine political squabbles, black churches remained a viable religious movement. The civil rights-black power movement provided a new setting for clarification of identity and mission. Thus, with the emergence of black theology, black churches were called again to renew their historical vocation. However, the context has changed. In the eighteenth and nineteenth centuries, the black church movement was largely a rural phenomenon. Increasingly since World War II, with the migration of Afro-Americans to urban areas, that setting has changed.

The New Context

Several years ago, while riding public transportation in Washington, D.C., I was privileged to overhear a conversation between two persons sitting behind me. While not generally given to eavesdropping, I could not help but become interested in this very delicate family crisis that was being discussed. Both persons were intensely emotional and seemed to be very intimately involved. After about twenty minutes of discussion, it was clear that they were not discussing a family situation, but rather an afternoon soap opera. I was fascinated. Here were two reasonably well-dressed, seemingly stable ladies, discussing a television show as though it were a real-life situation. I wondered, *What was the phenome-*

non that could get these ladies so emotionally involved in a situational fantasy until they in their minds literally spoke of the characters as though they were relatives? I was later to discover that the loyalty of the followers of such programming is so intense that even in my local barbershop persons had been asked to be quiet during these soap operas.

Television is the dominant medium of communication during this part of the twentieth century. The altering of common life by scientific advances and discoveries is epitomized by the revolution in communication brought on by television. More than simply a means of communication, however, television has changed the way we view the world, our personal relationships, and our neighbors. It has, in a word, become a way of life. Its formative influence is felt in all arenas, especially in entertainment, politics, education, and religion. I am particularly concerned over its effect on religion. Television, as all technology, has an agenda. Our easy acceptance of a particular technology without a critical evaluation of its agenda and metaphors may seriously alter the original intent. William F. Fore, in a recent study of television and religion, has pointed out the extent to which television has become a major factor in our lives.

> The average viewer watched about four hours and thirty minutes each day. This amounts to 31.5 hours per week or considerably more than a full day and night in every week of every month of every year.

> This single statistic means that aside from eating, sleeping and working, most people in America spend 80 percent of their entire lives in the world of television rather than the real world. Of course, television does not completely exclude the real world, but families watch more than 45 hours each week, in households with cable subscription services the figure increases to 58 hours, while most adults spend only 40 hours at work and children spend only 30 hours in school.[3]

Much information has been published on the ill effects that television has on children and teenagers. While these figures are generally true for the American majority, minorities, blacks in particular, watch more television than any other racial/ethnic group in this country. Until recently, however, few studies have moved beyond the pabulum that the industry puts out to investigate television as a cultural phenomenon. What are the effects of this medium of entertainment on culture, value, and faith in America? Have the television evangelists become the chief medium of evangelism in our days? Has television become the major storyteller of this half of the twentieth century? In addition to Fore's study published as *Television and Religion: The Shaping of Faith, Values, and Culture*, Neil Postman has presented some interesting observations in his *Amusing Ourselves to Death: Public Discourse in the Age of Show Business*.

Both Postman and Fore see television as a major factor in the changing of the American world view.[4] Postman argues that the dominance of television in the American public life has reduced all public discourse to trivia. Whether in religion, politics, or education, success is based not on ideas or authenticity, but on whether or not it sells on television. Postman is influenced by Aldous Huxley's prophecy of a political future in a brave new world. Thus he believes that television becomes the medium of control by satisfying "the human infinite appetite for distraction."[5] Fore, on the other hand, makes the assessment that television is a major shaper of world views and values. He admits that television has positive qualities. However, unlike Postman, Fore has based his conclusions on a study of television and its effects on religion, commissioned by the National Council of the Churches of Christ and the National Religious Broadcasters. The intent of the study was to gather information on the effects of "the electronic church" on mainline churches. The discoveries were interesting and instructive.

1. The viewing audience of the electronic church program were far smaller than claimed.
2. The electronic church is not effective evangelism, although it is an effective reinforcer of existing religious beliefs of viewers.

3. The roles of people are essentially the same in the symbolic worlds of both the electronic church programs and general television programs.
4. For most heavy viewers of religious television, watching the program is both an extension of belief and an act of protest against the world of general television.[6]

Far more telling than the results on the religious broadcasting was the research implying that the greatest threat to churches in America was not the television evangelist but general television itself.

It has already been noted that both Postman and Fore acknowledge that television plays a controlling role in how most Americans perceive reality. If then television is providing the language symbols and images that allow us to determine what we really are, what are the new images of this new medium?

One has only to look at television to discover that its world is a world of white middle-class, single males in their prime. These males generally possess all of the power. In television land, Fore observes, "If one happens to be a powerful white American, then the ends justify all kinds of means, and one is rewarded with TV's images of happiness."[7]

Over against the teachings of the Christian faith, television lifts images of survival of the fittest; power is concentrated in some central location, (such as Hollywood, Washington, or New York); happiness and success come with unlimited acquisition of things; and all progress is good.

The lifting of values follows the perspective that power is the most important value in television land. Not only should one have power over others, but one should also have power over nature. It is a small wonder then that the most popular television shows are those that portray persons of immense wealth and property buying anything they want, consuming only the best, and awash in creature comforts. Thus the viewer is to believe that happiness only can come with the acquisition of things, plus sex appeal, pride, and power over others.

Television does not stop there. Commercials that are supposed to sell us soap and cereals are making claims for their products that once were exclusively made by religion. Coca-Cola promises to bring the warring people of the earth to a hill in perfect harmony singing about and drinking Coke. It is, after all, *the real thing*. Thus, drinking Coca-Cola is now associated with a way of life and a world view. If, while one is watching television, one can engage the ideas intellectually, discuss them, and debate them with others, then perhaps one can make a decision to accept or reject. However, most television is watched in silence or while one is alone. The anchoring is completed before the individual can critically evaluate the content. Fore makes a significant point here.

> Individuals need to cultivate the ability to stand back and create aesthetic and intellectual "distance" between themselves and what they see on TV and then, from the critical perspective informed by their faith look at what television is doing and saying.[8]

The nature of television as a medium often does not allow persons to filter what is real and what is not. Early in Chapter 5 I noted that the difference between the imagination and the imaginary was that the imagination represents the constructive creative powers of the mind and the imaginary represents the unreal. The critical issue for millions of Americans, black and white, is not whether Gilligan's Island exists but whether the world view offered by television is real. Thomas Morgan shares the dilemma of black parents regarding this matter.

> Parents want to know how to help them establish a black identity and pride while they are learning white mainstream cultural values through the influence of television, popular music and friendship with whites.[9]

The tragedy is that most Americans, black or white, fail to recognize that the cultural world view of television is little more than fantasy. It is a world view of television land that exists only in the minds of those in places of power who develop and design the shows and the minds of many Americans whose filters of consciousness have not allowed them to place distance between themselves and what is viewed on television. Dr. Alvin Poussaint perceptively notes the following about the Cosby show.

> The most common reaction from whites has been "the show is great, Cosby is funny, but it's not real, is it? You're putting one over on us, right? Black families like that just don't exist."
>
> A lot of them seem to think that we are presenting these perfect role models that don't have any reality in the black community. I don't know that the Cosby family is any less realistic than any of the white families you see on sitcoms.[10]

Poussaint, of course, is correct. Cosby is about as realistic as the Ewings in "Dallas" or the Carringtons in "Dynasty." But a deeper truth lies in his comments. Namely, whites, including those who are supposedly critical, have started to believe that there really is such a place as Gilligan's Island.

My earlier response to the pastor friend is significant here. The tradition of spirituals and conversion stories is the story of a culture that used these media to pass on a world view, values, and beliefs to each succeeding generation. In an extremely hostile environment that sought to deny the slaves their humanity, they rejected the "thingification" classification and found in their religion a self-understanding that still defies rationality. Whatever the systematic enslavement attempted to do to them, it did not destroy their self-transcendence. It was a living tradition that was renewed with each succeeding generation. It also was a tradition that provided clarity of identity and a purposefulness of mission.

Since the early part of this century, the black American community has moved from one identity crisis to another. Wilmore has accurately described it as a cutoff from its roots. The term "new Negro" is a recurring phrase that seeks to identify the aspirations of the black middle class assimilation hopes in many generations. As early as 1896 the Rev. John T. C. Newsome observed:

> Contemporaneously with the new South, the new Negro has appeared on the scene, the Negro born of schools and colleges and bent more on acquiring a home, amassing wealth, and the improvement of the social condition of his home, than the support of the grog shop, the gambling hall and other institutions of idleness.[11]

Critical for both the urban black poor and the upwardly mobile middle-class black professional is the current identity crisis. While the present crisis is identity, it is not peculiar to black Americans. All Americans suffer from a weakening of the traditional underpinning brought on by technology, but it is uniquely acute among black Americans already denied access to the American mainstream. Lacking the traditional mooring for self-understanding and emotional support, the urban poor and upwardly mobile middle-class professional blacks have turned to the world of television. They are seeking a definition of reality and self-understanding from a medium that is inherently steeped in preserving the status quo and stereotypical views of minorities. Such an investment is destructive, since success as defined by American television is to be white or acceptable to whiteness. This dependence is played out absurdly through conspicuous consumption that can only be described as "name brand madness." The urban poor person views material possession as a declaration of somebodiness. The same is true for the black middle-class counterpart for whom price tags are bigger, items different, but the symptoms the same. It seems to me the apparent chasm between the urban poor black and the upwardly mobile one is neither that wide nor is it unbridgeable. Both have been perpetually shut out of the mainstream of American political, social, economic, and religious life. Each daily faces subtle and overt assaults on dignity and personhood.

These factors, coupled with the loss of a sense of community in impersonal urban America, have fostered widespread alienation. Claude Brown makes the point forcefully.

One youngster told me he lost interest in school when teachers had no obvious interest in instructing him. "It's about knowing somebody cares," he said. "That's what makes you care."[12]

Over against this hunger of the heart is the healing, liberating, transforming word from the gospel. The good news is that the searing estrangement felt by this youngster from Harlem and countless others, I believe, is an expression of a deep, abiding search for wholeness. To this hunger of the heart comes a healing, liberating, transforming word that is from the gospel and the story of his people. The word of good news is that God cares. In times past, God's providential care has been sustaining and evidenced in the lives of this youngster's forebears. Furthermore, the good news is what God has done in the past, God will do again even if it is under changing circumstances. One suspects the real tragedy is that it is a story he has not yet heard. That this story has not yet been communicated to him and countless others like him, young and old, poor and middle class, represents a major challenge for black churches in this latter part of the twentieth century.

The present context has weakened seriously the traditional mooring of the black church movement. To recapture their vitality and passion, black churches must recover their foundational stories. They must recall, again, God's activity among the founders of the black religious tradition. To retell that story is to give new meaning, power, and passion to the spiritual descendants of George Liele, Richard Allen, James Varick, and others. God's saving and liberating activity among the beginners empowered and equipped them to become an evangelizing, caring, and supportive family. They carried a word of liberation and reconciliation to their brothers and sisters. To recall that is to recall the story of God's reign in the lives of black Americans. It is the story of God among us. It is God's story. It is also our story. To suggest that the foundational story has no relevance is to suggest that the black church movement cling perpetually to its current identity crisis, moving with "every wind that blows."

The Challenge of the Future

The story of one church, Missionary Union Church (Baptist),* offers some insight into the challenges facing black congregations.

Missionary Union Church has a large congregation of four-thousand-plus members. It is dually aligned with the American Baptist Churches in the U.S.A. and the National Baptist Convention, U.S.A., Incorporated. The church is centrally located in its home city along a major traffic corridor. While portions of the immediate neighborhood surrounding the church have become blighted, located adjacent to the church is a major medical complex and a large university. Very few members of the congregation live in the community. The church, however, is actively involved in its home area. Its physical plant provides ample facilities for the many outreach ministries sponsored and/or participated in by the church. They include a food pantry/thrift shop, tutorial services, scouting, counseling, day care, Meals on Wheels, athletic activities, and adult education programs.

Within the congregation a small but vocal minority continually has pestered the leadership about a perceived lack of commitment to evangelism. The senior minister, seeking to be responsive, has assigned an associate minister and a member of the board of deacons to work with this group. It was decided that an evangelism Bible study group would be formed. The church staff sought help from American Baptists to teach the class.

Problems surfaced within the group almost immediately. Differing expectations, sporadic attendance, and smoldering hostility toward the church's leadership nearly disrupted the group. By the fifth session attendance had stabilized, expectations had been renegotiated, and the anger had been placed on the table and vented.

Persons began to work on seeing and hearing their stories in preparation for a visitation program. Interestingly, the group decided that its members were not ready to begin calling; something needed to be done to heighten

*Missionary Union Church (Baptist) is a fictitious name although the story is real.

the congregation's awareness of the importance of visitation. Members decided to become greeters for the Sunday worship service during the summer interim when the class was not meeting. The pastor recognized the group's ministry from the pulpit and introduced the new greeters to the congregation. Members of the congregation who had never been greeted were ecstatic. So effective was this ministry of hospitality that new volunteers enlarged the group for the fall sessions. Members of the original group were buoyed by this; they now were ready to become involved in visitation. During the fall sessions the group worked on developing a visitation list beginning with visitors. The church currently has an evangelism visitation program.

The Missionary Union Church story highlights several crucial issues for many churches.

Pastoral leadership—The pastoral leadership, while leading a dynamic church in mission, did not really validate evangelism as a part of the overall mission of the church. Those interested in that ministry felt pushed aside to be involved in busywork that really did not go anywhere. Members understood what ministries were held in high regard; theirs was not. Their anger and resentment were directed toward the associate minister, the deacon, and the instructor. Once the work of the group was validated by the senior minister, the attitudes of the group participants changed.

Planning—Virtually no planning had gone into the development of this ministry. It was an attempt, at best, to be responsive to what was perceived as a developing crisis. Planning would have required thinking through how evangelism fit into the total mission of the church as well as preparing the congregation to support a ministry of evangelism. The leadership later acknowledged that the study-group approach was a kind of afterthought. The church's leadership, interestingly, has a history of carefully thought-out and planned projects in ministry.

The issue of spontaneity—The matter of planning raised another critical issue that must be held in tension with intentionality—spontaneity. For many in black churches, any attempt to plan, set goals or objectives represents an effort to quench the Spirit. It is true that there are those in the church for whom planning represents an end in itself rather than a means to an end. There are, within my own denomination, many church leaders and local congregations for whom thinking, reading, talking, and rallying about the work of evangelism becomes an excuse for not being an evangelist. Black churches, on the other hand, should avoid the pitfalls of this excess. However, planning should never be shunted aside. The new context in which we find ourselves requires that planning and the spontaneous be held in tension. Prayerfully thinking projects through and searching for God's direction in all of its work is not alien to the black religious experience. The winds of the Spirit will blow as they will. We in the church must trim our sails so that when the wind does blow we will be blessed. Some of the persons attending sessions seriously believed that all that was needed was willing hearts and the group was ready to go calling in the neighborhood.

Cultivating lay leadership—One of the reasons for sporadic attendance during initial sessions of the group was that many of the original participants were heavily involved in other groups within the congregation. They were interested in evangelism, but were simply overworked. They wanted to support this ministry, but there were not enough hours or days nor enough stamina to be involved in everything. The leadership was reluctant to insist on attendance. Moreover, they refused to give those persons whose gifts were invaluable in other areas permission not to participate. The instructor had to force the issue. Here was a congregation of four thousand persons, with a small circle of persons carrying all of the leadership responsibility. Most of the active membership simply was not involved. When the group became greeters and received official recognition in the morning service, volunteers sought out the group to join.

Caring-supportive congregation—Missionary Union Church uses "a friendly church" as one of its slogans. There were many small groups within the congregation for whom this slogan was true. For those within the leadership circle, this was especially true. However, to the newcomer or the visitors who simply walked in, one could attend several services without being greeted at all. Even members of the study group did not really believe their congregation was friendly. Many expressed concern that persons from the neighborhood surrounding the church might not feel welcome. Missionary Union is what is commonly called within the black American community a "silk stocking church." Such congregations are decidedly middle class, though many would prefer to be called cross-sectional. Worshipers who do not dress like the majority of the congregation are generally screened out. When participants in the evangelism study group began serving as greeters, they were unable to distinguish visitors from regular members. They greeted everyone. The response within the congregation was tremendous. Greeters were able to share personal stories told by members who were excited by the hospitality. Their concerns about a large congregation's ability to be a caring community were altered. Additionally, consciousness raising occurred for the congregation.

A caring-supportive congregation is important to the work of evangelism. The two complement each other. Without a nurturing-caring fellowship, regardless of how much evangelism is done, the congregation becomes a revolving door.

Empowering members to tell their stories—The most crucial task in the evangelism group was to get in touch with how God has and does work in their own lives and to be able to share their story. Several members of the group felt that their stories did not count. They were willing to use "religious talk." Religious talk comprises those popular, nice, pious clichés used regularly by church members. No one really knows what they mean, but everyone is supposed to know, so no one ever asks. Others in the group were willing to tell someone else's story. Once past the religious talk, members were able to recall significant experiences of God's work in their lives. The authority of personal experiences was validated. As members became aware of the work of the Spirit in their own lives, they began to speak with integrity about their experiences to others. They listened and were listened to. As they listened to other stories, they were able to discern the activity of God in the lives of other members of the group. This required, for some, a change in attitude and discipline. In speaking and listening to one another, relationships were developed and enhanced.

Many of the stories were on themes that could be traced to the history of Missionary Union Church. As participants saw and heard their own stories, they felt better about themselves and the church.

While Missionary Union has an illustrious history that seemingly informs some of its present mission activity, the church does not tell its corporate story. Even in its new member classes, new congregants are not given the story. A brief biography of the church in a souvenir program provides a chronicle of pastoral and building changes, as though this church's rich tradition of involvement in the transformation of its community could be reduced to pastoral leadership changes or bricks and mortar. Though involved in mission outreach, Missionary Union had become an insular community. Until recently, it did not recruit members. It has lost the passion of its founders and the beginners of the Afro-American religious experience to share the good news of the gospel with persons outside the fellowship. Even though there are persons who are recipients of the mission outreach of the church, many using its buildings are not invited to become a part of this community of faith. What is true of Missionary Union is true of many churches. This church may be the rule rather than the exception. To be able to recall the tradition of spirituals and conversion stories would allow for the recapture of some of the lost vitality of this church.

In preparation for a consultation on Old First churches within American Baptist churches, fifty churches were asked, among other things, to recall the original vision of the founders. Some gave chronicles that related to buildings, budgets, and pastors. Others were able to see their churches in the context of a larger environment. Each was able to share how recalling the vitality of the foundational story was a source of renewal.

Seeing and Hearing Your Story

The ability to see and hear your own story is not as difficult as you may think. It does, however, require intentionality. Our lack of good stories in the present context allows the imagination to become rusty from disuse. I want to suggest two processes for you to follow that will overcome the veils that life's intensity places over our stories.

I. Reflection: My Faith Story

Each person who seeks to be an evangelist can learn much about evangelism by reflecting on his or her spiritual journey.

1. How did I come to my personal experience of Jesus Christ?

2. Who or what experience brought me into the church?

3. What activities of the church bring me my greatest joy?

4. What lets me know that I belong to this church? (How do I know I'm included; that I'm cared for?)

5. What does that caring feel like?

6. What keeps me Christian?

II. My Theological Autobiography

Every story has meaning. We find the meaning for our lives in story.

1. *Meditation and prayer.* Find a quiet place and center down; that is, calm all of the physical and mental noises within that distract your ability to wait in silence. It is important to relax and ignore the impulse to do something. Allow the emptying of the mind to simply happen to you (a simple breathing exercise will help).
2. *Slowly read a passage of Scripture.* Allow the insight about the people, events, characters, and experiences to come to you. Let them speak to you. What would it have been like to be an eyewitness, a hearer, an original reader?
3. *Allow the text to remind you* of one or two persons whom you know. Recall specific stories about these people. What has it been like to know these people?
4. *Pray for the persons,* thank them, and let them go.
5. *Continue your pilgrimage* into your personal history. Recall a time in your life when you were afraid and someone or something gave you courage, were burdened and forgiveness came, were lonely and someone came and cared for you. What was that moment? How did it feel? Play back the memory tape.
6. *Pray for that person,* thank him or her, and let him or her go.

You now have a story that came out of your life. You may want to write it down. Whether you record it or not, it is important to remember this precious gift. As we recall the experiences of God's involvement in our lives, the story grabs us at the feeling level and we know that this is a good story. We know also that it is fragmented, part of a larger story. God's story. Our stories are not simply for our personal reflection. Indeed, it is only in the sharing of stories that we celebrate the victories and are healed by sharing the pain. This is done in community. The sharing reflects the images and symbols of the community. As we make connection with others and their stories, we are also connected with the life-giving and life-transforming story of the gospel.

The gospel story, the story of the community, and your story are all good stories. Good stories capture and hold the attention of the listener. When we hear good stories we know in the very depths of our being that this story is true, that it is my story also.

Evangelism in black churches has always been the telling of the story, the story of Jesus, the story of a people, the personal story of individuals. In its finest moments, those stories have been shared to transform communities and lives. At other times denial and substitutions of the story created perpetual identity crises.

Now that you have recovered your story, remember, *stories are for telling!*

Notes

Chapter 1

1 James H. Cone, *God of the Oppressed* (New York: The Seabury Press, Inc.), p. 102.

2 Albert J. Raboteau, *Slave Religion: The "Invisible Institution" in the Antebellum South* (New York: Oxford University Press, Inc., 1978), p. 6.

3 See quote of Lawrence A. Jones in his "They Sought a City" on page 9 in C. Eric Lincoln, ed., *The Black Experience in Religion* (Garden City, New York: Anchor Press/Doubleday, 1974), pp. 7–23.

4 Winthrop D. Jordan, White over Black American Attitudes Toward the Negro 1550–1812 (New York: W. W. Norton and Company, Inc., 1977), p. 212.

Chapter 2

1 Justo L. Gonzalez, *A History of Christian Thought*, vol. 3: *From the Protestant Reformation to the Twentieth Century* (Nashville: Abingdon Press, 1975), pp. 274–279.

2 Donald G. Mathews, *Religion in the Old South* (Chicago: The University of Chicago Press, 1977), pp. xvi-xviii.

3 See Albert J. Raboteau, *Slave Religion*, pp. 97–128.

4 William B. McClain, *Black People in the Methodist Church: Whither Thou Goest?* (Cambridge: Schenkman Publishing Company, Inc., 1984), pp. 21–37.

5 Mathews, *Old South*, p. 190.

6 *Ibid.*, pp. 190–192.

7 See McClain, *Black People*, pp. 21–37; Mathews, *Old South*, pp. 194–195.

8 McClain, *Black People*, pp. 20–21.

9 *Ibid.*, pp. 31–54.

10 Gayraud S. Wilmore, *Black Religion and Black Radicalism: An Interpretation of the Religious History of Afro-American People*, sec. ed., (Maryknoll, New York: Orbis Books, 1983), pp. 120–122. See entire Chapter 5, "Black Religion and Black Radicalism," pp. 99–134.

11 See the quote of Richard Allen in his "Life Experience and Gospel Labors," on page 141 in Milton C. Sernett's edited work *Afro-American Religious History: A Documentary Witness* (Durham: Duke University Press, 1985). See also pp. 141–142.

12 *Ibid.*, p. 142.

13 Clarence E. Walker, *A Rock in a Weary Land: The African Methodist Episcopal Church During the Civil War and Reconstruction* (Baton Rouge: Louisiana State University Press, 1982), pp. 1–2.

14 William Jacob Walls, *The African Methodist Episcopal Church: Reality of the Black Church* (Charlotte: A.M.E. Zion Publishing House, 1974), pp. 133–135.

15 L.L. Berry, *A Century of Missions of the African Methodist Episcopal Church 1840–1940* (New York: Gutenberg Printing Co., Inc., 1942), p. 45.

16 *Ibid.*, p. 49.

17 James Melvin Washington, *Frustrated Fellowship: The Black Baptist Quest for Social Power* (Macon: Mercer University Press, 1986), pp. 27–43.

18 *Ibid.*, pp. 32–33.

19 Leroy Fitts, *A History of Black Baptists* (Nashville: Broadman Press, 1985), pp. 109–112.

20 Raboteau, *Slave Religion*, pp. 139–140.

21 See Sandy Dwayne Martin's "Black Baptists, Foreign Missions, and African Colonization, 1814–1882" in Sylvia M. Jacobs, ed., *Black Americans and the Missionary Movement in Africa* (Westport, Conn.: Greenwood Press, 1982), pp. 63–76.

22 Berry, *Century*, p. 91.

23 Walker, *Rock*, pp. 19, 137.

24 Walls, *AMEZ*, p. 228.

25 See Allen's quote in David Walker's *Appeal in Four Articles* (39–117) printed in Sterling Stuckey, ed., *The Ideological Origins of Black Nationalism* (Boston: Beacon Press, 1972), p. 94.

26 *Ibid.*, for example, pp. 53–59, 75, 77.

27 *Ibid.*, pp. 55–56.

28 *Ibid.*, p. 56.

29 *Ibid.*, p. 56.

30 *Ibid.*, p. 57.

31 *Ibid.*, footnote 1, p. 57.

32 *Ibid.*, p. 59.

33 Frederick Douglass's quote comes from p. 104 in his "Slaveholding Religion and the Christianity of Christ" (100–109) printed in Sernett's *Afro-American.*

34 See Henry Highland Garnet's "An Address to the Slaves of the United States . . . ," pp. 165–173 in Stuckey, *Ideological*. The quote is on page 168.

35 *Ibid.*

Chapter 3

1 See Raboteau, *Slave Religion*, and Lawrence W. Levine, *Black Culture and Black Consciousness: Afro-American Folk Thought from Slavery to Freedom* (New York: Oxford University Press, Inc., 1977).

2 See "Autobiography 1: The Slave Who Joined the Yanks," pp. 24–57 in Clifton H. Johnson, ed., *God Struck Me Dead: Religious Conversion Experiences and Autobiographies of Ex-Slaves* (New York: The Pilgrim Press, 1969). See quote on p. 45.

3 *Ibid.*, pp. 45–46.

4 Levine, *Black Culture*, p. 44.

5 *Ibid.*, p. 37.

6 Edward F. and Anne Streaty Wimberly, *Liberation and Human Wholeness:*

The Conversion Experiences of Black People in Slavery and Freedom (Nashville: Abingdon Press, 1986), pp. 70–71.

7 Levine, *Black Culture*, p. 42.

8 Wimberly, *Liberation*, pp. 90–91.

9 Raboteau, *Slave Religion*.

10 Wimberly, *Liberation*, pp. 28–31.

11 Wimberly, *Liberation*, p. 30.

12 *Ibid.*, p. 3.

13 *Ibid.*, pp. 30–35. See also Raboteau, *Slave Religion*, pp. 211–288; Levine, *Black Culture*, pp. 33–80.

14 Levine, *Black Culture*, see quote on p. 33. See also pp. 30–80.

15 Washington, *Fellowship*, p. 61.

16 Bishop Daniel Alexander Payne, *Recollections of Seventy Years*, edited by C. S. Smith. (New York: Arno Press and *The New York Times*, 1968), pp. 161–163.

17 *Ibid.*, p. 162.

18 *Ibid.*, pp. 162–163.

19 See William Jones, *Is God a White Racist?* (New York: Doubleday and Co., Inc., 1973).

20 Walls, *AMEZ*, pp. 186–187, 189. See also Carter G. Woodson, *The History of the Negro Church*, third ed. (Washington, D.C.: The Associated Publishers, 1972), Chapter 11, "The Call of Politics," pp. 198–223 for a survey of black ministers' involvement in post-Civil War politics.

21 Washington, *Fellowship*, pp. 60–61.

22 Walker, *Rock*, pp. 15–16.

23 Litwack, *Storm*, pp. 450–501.

24 *Ibid.*, p. 458.

25 *Ibid.*, pp. 450–501.

26 *Ibid.*, p. 460.

27 For accounts on the black church and African missions, see Sylvia M. Jacobs, ed., Black Americans; and Sandy D. Martin, "The Growth of Christian Missionary Interest in West Africa Among Southeastern Black Baptists, 1880–1915." (Unpublished Ph.D. dissertation, Columbia University, 1981).

28 See Fitts, *Black Baptists*, pp. 112–120; and Sandy Dwayne Martin, "The Baptist Foreign Mission Convention," *Baptist History and Heritage*, 16 (October 1981), p. 13–25 for accounts of black Baptists' African missions programs in the post-Civil War era.

29 Fitts, *Black Baptists*, p. 116.

30 See Walls, *AMEZ*, pp. 189, 230–238 for a discussion of African mission among the Zionites.

31 *Ibid.*, p. 238.

32 See Berry, *Century*, pp. 149–156 for an account of African missions among the AME.

33 For the debate between Nazery and Payne, see *Ibid.*, pp. 55–57.

34 *Ibid.*, p. 57.

35 *Ibid.*, pp. 103–104.

36 For a treatment of Turner, African emigration, and African evangelization, see Walker, *Rock*, pp. 127–138.

37 Two good sources on the rise of gospel music are Laurraine Goreau, *Just Mahalia Baby: The Mahalia Jackson Story* (Gretna, Louisiana: Pelican Publishing Company, Inc., 1984; originally published Waco, Texas: Word Books, 1975); *Sacred Music and Social Change* (Valley Forge: Judson Press, 1979). See especially Chapter 7 in Walker's book, "The Lord Will Make a Way Somehow! Gospel: Historic and Modern," pp. 127–172.

Chapter 4

1 Alex Haley, *Roots* (New York: Doubleday and Co., Inc., 1976), pp. 674–675.

2 Yves M. J. Congar, *Tradition and Traditions: An Historical and Theological Essay* (New York: Macmillan Publishing Company, 1967), p. 5.

3 J. Albert Soggin, *Introduction to the Old Testament* (Philadelphia: The Westminster Press, 1974), p. 59.

4 *Ibid.*, p. 59.

5 Haley, *Roots*, p. 674.

6 See S. Mowinckel, "Oral Tradition," in *The Interpreter's Dictionary of the Bible*, vol. 4, (Nashville: Abingdon Press, 1962), pp. 683–685.

7 As quoted in Levine, *Black Culture*, p. 4.

8 Washington, *Fellowship*, p. x.

9 Levine, *Black Culture*, p. 5.

10 Richard Bandler and John Grinder, *The Structure of Magic: A Book on Language and Therapy* (Palo Alto, Calif.: Science and Behavior Books, Inc., 1975), p. 13.

11 Mircea Eliade, *Patterns in Comparative Religions* (New York: Sheed and Ward, 1958), p. 454.

12 Henry H. Mitchell, *The Recovery of Preaching* (New York: Harper and Row, Publishers Inc., 1977), p. 16.

13 Raboteau, *Slave Religion*, p. 121.

14 *Ibid.*, p. 121.

15 See quote of Aldous Huxley in Bandler and Grinder, *Structure of Magic*, pp. 9–10.

16 Mitchell, *Preaching*, p. 19.

17 See John S. Mbiti, *African Religions and Philosophy* (Garden City, New York: Anchor Books, 1970), Chapter 3, pp. 19–36, and Chapter 7, pp. 75–96.

18 Levine, *Black Culture*, p. 31.

19 Raboteau, *Slave Religion*, p. 238.

20 *Ibid.*, p. 208.

21 *Ibid.*, p. 228.

22 *Ibid.*, p. 239.

23 *Ibid.*, pp. 239–243.

24 *Ibid.*

Chapter 5

1 William F. Fore, *Television and Religion: The Shaping of Faith, Values, and Culture* (Minneapolis: Augsburg Press, 1987), p. 55.

2 As quoted in Stanley Haverwas' *Truthfulness and Tragedy* (Notre Dame: University of Notre Dame Press, 1977), pp. 71–72.

3 Raboteau, *Slave Religion*, pp. 243–265. See also Levine, *Black Culture*, pp. 30–55; Eileen Southern; *The Music of Black Americans: A History*, sec. ed. (New York: W. W. Norton and Company Inc., 1970,) pp. 150–188; Howard Thurman, *Deep River* (Richmond, Ind.: Friends United Press, 1975).

4 *Ibid.*, p. 259.

5 Private collection.

6 Thurman, *Deep River*, p. 70.

7 *Ibid.*, p. 19.

8 *Ibid.*, p. 20.

9 *Ibid.*, p. 21.

10 Quoted tape conversations with Howard Thurman and ten seminary students. Recorded February 1980.

11 John Dunne, *Time and Myth* (Notre Dame: University of Notre Dame Press, 1975), p. 100.

12 Urban T. Holmes III, *Ministry and Imagination* (New York: The Seabury Press, 1981), p. 180.

Chapter 6

1 Washington, *Fellowship*, p. 150.

2 See quote in "Introduction to Black Theology and the Black Church," by Gayraud S. Wilmore, p. 245. Gayraud S. Wilmore and James H. Cone, eds., *Black Theology: A Documentary History 1966–1979* (Maryknoll, N.Y.: Orbis Books, 1979), pp. 241–256.

3 Fore, *Religion and Television*, p. 16.

4 See Postman, *Amusing Ourselves to Death*, and Fore, *Religion and Television*.

5 Neil Postman, *Amusing Ourselves to Death: Public Discourse in the Age of Show Business* (New York: The Viking Press, 1985), p. VIII.

6 Fore, *Religion and Television*, pp. 98–114.

7 *Ibid.*, p. 64.

8 *Ibid.*, p. 68.

9 Thomas Morgan, "The World Ahead," *The New York Times Magazine*, October 27, 1985, p. 34.

10 As quoted in Ellen Hopkins, "Blacks at the Top," *New York Magazine*, January 19, 1987, p. 23.

11 Washington, *Fellowship*, p. 197.

12 Claude Brown, "Manchild in Harlem," *The New York Times Magazine*, September 19, 1984, p. 77.